Maps & Legends
Poems to Find Your Way By

Maps & Legends
Poems to Find Your Way By

Edited by Jo Bell and Jane Commane

ISBN: 978-0-9573847-5-0

First published December 2013 by:

Nine Arches Press
PO Box 6269
Rugby
CV21 9NL
United Kingdom

www.ninearchespress.com

Printed in Britain by:

imprintdigital.net
Seychelles Farm,
Upton Pyne,
Exeter
EX5 5HY
www.imprintdigital.net

Maps & Legends
Poems to Find Your Way By

Edited by Jo Bell
and Jane Commane

Nine
Arches
Press

ABOUT THE EDITORS

Jo Bell is a former Glastonbury Poet in Residence and director of National Poetry Day – a post she recently left to become the UK's first Canal Laureate. A boat-dweller and former archaeologist, she has been published in journals from *Magma* and *Popshot* to the *Frogmore Papers*, and appeared at festivals from Shambala to Cheltenham Literature Festival. Her current projects include Wordsmiths & Co, a poetry talk show at Warwick Arts Centre, and her most recent collection is *Navigation*.

Jane Commane is editor at Nine Arches Press and *Under the Radar* magazine, a poet, and a freelance writing tutor. Her poetry has been published widely in magazines and journals, including *Tears in the Fence, The Warwick Review, Iota, Anon* and *The Morning Star*. Her poems have been collected in several anthologies, including *The Best British Poetry 2011* (Salt Publishing) and *Lung Jazz: Young British Poets for Oxfam* (Cinnamon Press). As well as poetry, Jane has worked in museum education and archive conservation. She lives and works in Warwickshire.

CONTENTS

FOREWORD

This is a birthday gala of poetry from Nine Arches Press, in a publication marking their fifth year of life. The poems offer a range of maps and legends – the tales, the landmarks, the emotional charts by which we navigate.

In the ancient world, infant mortality was very high. If you made it past your fifth birthday and the worst dangers of illness or circumstance, you were likely to make it into adulthood with its different perils. In the world of poetry publishing too, many a hopeful young press is snatched away before it gets a chance to grow strong. The establishment of a poetry imprint is always a sign of touching faith and optimism, some would say of foolishness; all the more reason to celebrate the sturdy youngster that is Nine Arches Press.

Nine Arches launched their first pamphlet in October 2008. A series of beautiful, powerful short collections followed it, including Roz Goddard's *The Sopranos Sonnets and Other Poems*, based on the TV programme, and Tony Williams' extraordinary, fragmented visual poetry in *All the Rooms of Uncle's Head* (reproduced towards the end of this book). Since 2009, full-length titles have followed. Dozens of publications later, the patient commitment of editor Jane Commane (and co-editor Matt Nunn from 2008-12) has paid off.

Nine Arches share an appetite for plain but playful language, as shown in Simon Turner's 'Digital Birmingham'; an eye for poetry that romps unexpectedly on the page like David Morley's 'Moolò the Musician', and for the formal accomplishment of Angela France's 'Canzone: Cunning'; an ear for wit as Luke Kennard demonstrates. Above all, Nine Arches has an unfailing loyalty to the English Midlands which a number of their poets call home. This connection to a homeland is key to their identity and their choices. The books, though varied, have a familial sense of kith and kin; a tang of the Mercian.

Always read the disclaimer, says Tom Chivers in his 'A Guide to Email Etiquette' – and he's right, of course. So here is ours: this selection is, by definition, not completely exhaustive. It's a tasting menu from the range of Nine Arches titles, giving a sample of their work so far. Some of these, like Phil Brown, are newly published; others, like David Hart, long-established. The selection includes those who like to experiment with form and style, like Chris McCabe or Tom Chivers; the intense miniaturist observations of David Morley and Matt Merritt; the appetite for whimsy seen in Deborah Tyler-Bennett's poems.

All have enjoyed a rare kind of dedication from their publisher and editor. The relationship between writer and editor is an intimate one. A good editor builds a relationship with a writer, allowing the poetry to grow in sometimes unexpected directions and encouraging new poets to test their own voice in a safe space. Angela France, for instance, first published by Nine Arches in her pamphlet *Lessons in Mallemaroking*, emerges as fully-formed poet in her collection *Hide*. The continuity of relationship gave her space to develop a strong and distinctive voice.

Enjoy the poems, and partake of the birthday feast – for without you at the table, dear reader, there would be no party. Celebrate the continuity and the generous spirit of Nine Arches, and join me in hoping that this will be the first of many such collections.

Jo Bell
November 2013.

PHIL BROWN

STAGE FRIGHT

Do not buy a beautiful notebook
with the hope of coaxing beautiful thoughts
onto the page as if all they needed
was a well-lit stage on which to flourish.

Buy the book by all means but be warned
that your thoughts will shrivel and cower
until there is no beautifully-bound
cahier and no mellifluous fountain pen.

Accept that the only real poetry
has its first airing on the backs
of bus tickets, or the margins
of newspapers, or if you have a real

opus on your hands, then that is
where you must write it;
on your hands. You will never
have a great meal in the most

expensive restaurant, and the plushest
hotel rooms will always be
conducive to bad sex. So throw
away your moleskines and let the poems

loose, let them infect the fodder
of your wallets and pockets
and napkins and tickets, plant them
where it is dark enough to grow.

DIPTYCH

Across

2. Campus in a wasteland (10)
6. A town hid in for a weekend (10)
7. Paper I scour for horoscopes (5)
9. A meal blackened in an oven (5)
11. The girl living on the floor above (4)
12. A disapproving brother (6)
14. Old ballroom in the midlands (3,3,5)
15. A train station I avoid now (6)
18. A book filled with photos of cats (1,3,3,11)
19. The girls' school that broke you (10)

Down

1. A dessert we shared (5,6)
3. The end of the Picadilly Line (8)
4. The town that took you back (5)
5. The boy who waited there for you (5)
8. A poem written on a postcard (3,3)
10. A restaurant in an airport (4,5)
13. A number on a door (8)
14. A song you sing better than the original (4,3)
17. A form filled in when the trouble started (5,3,7)
20. Something unsolvable (2)

ZUGSWANG

Her cuckold
who hasn't a clue

that she sleeps with her phone
on one side and me
on the other, and that
one night while she slept

I reached over, and made
a note of his number.

No idea of what depends
on the drunken vindictiveness
of a young man across the sea.
Would I want to know if it were me?

Her cuckold who hasn't a clue
but loves with his whole self.

A MAN NAMED ADAM

It starts with a man named Adam,
bald at twenty, good looking;
it's the eyes that do it,
he had the eyes of a little girl.

It starts in what was once
a retirement home. Converted, rented
by twenty strangers. Same décor
and sense of the terminal though.

It starts in the 'smoking-lounge'
(two chairs in a cellar)
and Adam needing a light
which I had.

It starts when I mention I'm broke
and those little-girl eyes of his
widen like a wine-stain
asking if I'd like a bit of work.

It starts a long time before any of that
but we have to start somewhere.

FIRST ABSTRACT CONCEPT

The stars are dimmer
here; *The*   *London Lite*
says it's   light
pollution,   but I
know it's   just reluctance
to acknowledge   the dead.
I see the   plough glint,
even when buried between *Tooting Bec* and *Broadway*. It is
clearer to me than street lamps, kebab-shop signs, than
headlights.   At seven
I learnt   my first
abstract concept,   it was
death, imminent   and beautiful.
At twenty-   one I
sit waiting   impatiently
for my stop.

PETER CARPENTER

FROM THE SMOKERY

Through the miracle of the smokery
it comes out fresh on the enamel plate
a full forty years on, stinking the place
to high heaven. I turn it from pipistrelle
to a woman's leather gloves to giant insect –
a stag beetle, cleavered, legs in the air, opening up
like a good short story.
                  Its armoury of bones
and deflector shields is surely cast in bronze.
A spine to work under and lift clear
with the line of the knife before the flesh
can be enjoyed: the intricacies of a whole life,
worth taking time over.
                  My long-dead grandfather
puts it there in front of me. Windows run
with condensation. The grill's still on for toast.
I make a start as he's creasing flat his *Mirror*.

KEITH STANDING

Field mushroom ears. Monday's callus of snot
or mashed potato still there on frayed Aertex collar come Friday.
John Lennon specs bleared by fingerprints, ice-rink scoured;
basin crewcut, involuntary half-grin, right arm braced permanently
in the air. Class fall guy, back-up anarchist when General Science
with Doc Death had passed its sell-by date.

'Sir, sir, I've swallowed some copper sulphate, sir.'

A frothy lisp of ocean-blue cola. Epsom District. Sirens, the works.

You grew on us. A trouper. For P.E. repeated offence:
coal-dust socks, no House vest. Punishment: in sheeting rain
to pick flints off terraced pitches down at Priest Hill. Undaunted,
you deliver them in a sack to Norris's desk like Millet's Sower
in steamed-over cartoon specs. Every day, arm aloft, the grin.
'Erm someone else... no, not you, Standing.'

'Sir, sir, I've got a rubber stuck up my nose, sir.'

But here's a question for you, Keith – how did it go? Not
the extraction of that tough khaki-green lozenge, but all those
after school activities – your late teens, employment, raising
a family, bank statements, the long haul, your life?

You can put your hand down now.

ORION

You have to see me to believe me or so I'm told.
I was up there when Dorothy was writing her journal:
Moonlight lay upon the hills like snow.
                                            Examine me now
and remember how your father fixed my position
in his calculations over Essen before the incendiary drop.
He thought I'd gone, but I came back for him years later,
unceremonious, no big deal, after that poached egg
on toast he'd fancied and a Sunday repeat of *Morse*.
On his side of the bed I touched him – sent him tumbling
past the face of the alarm clock, luminous, circa half
four in the morning. Had he been able to part the curtains
he'd have spotted me back up there, a nonchalant thief
on a clear night lining up for the identity parade, ready
to hold his gaze as sirens and blue flashing lights broke the peace.

SWEETMAN

Provider of bonbons, wine gums and lemon sherbets
from grease-proof paper bags stowed in the inside pocket
of a quilted anorak, thus christened 'Sweetman' by us,

located in E-Block mid-terrace regardless of
opposition (Grimsby in the Cup, their lads chanting 'Fishermen,
Fishermen, Fishermen', Wolves, Man City, the Baggies…),

which evening game was it that you melted away from,
long-striding it after a nil-one reverse, feeling in
anonymous sugar-dust for another predictable mouthful?

GIFT

after a line by Mandelstahm

A body. My very own possession –
what am I to make of you?
Devoted life-partner, let me know
who to thank. Involuntary father

confessor to my thousand secrets –
the crop circles of eczema,
the crisis of thinning hair –
comforter through night terrors,

you give me the freedom
to hold up a finger, thus,

and say I touch the sky.

TOM CHIVERS

A Guide to Email Etiquette

Don't reply to an email when angry, as you may regret it later.
Don't type in capitals as this is considered SHOUTING.
Don't send large attachments without checking with the
  recipient first.
Don't send chain letters or 'make money fast' messages.
Don't criticize spelling (sic.). It is considered petty.
Read the rules.
Don't flame people.
Don't make personal remarks.
Don't send unsuitable email.
Don't mention Lilly's hieroglyph.
Don't overuse the exclamation mark.
Be concise and to the point.
Don't reply to spam.
Don't gape at Puppet-shews.
Don't talk about the Press.
Don't excavate the ragstone.
Do not request delivery receipts.
Decode the spiel from 12 bit cant.
Do not make libellous, sexist or racially discriminating comments.
The Editors gave their reasons.

Sending email is like sending a postcard. Don't send it.
Brand the convict on his thumb.

You are using valuable bandwidth.
Do not covet ANY THING.
Spend your bounty-money where you can.

Always read the disclaimer.

Will, take out your field notebook. Make a tryst in blood. Employ your canines. Watch a shank of lamb slip off the bone as a woman stepping from her dress. This steaming viand, in its scrambled mess of lentils (puy), requires your total 100% concentration. I give you 'The Huntsman's Supper', or some other peasant chic moniker.

And while the bodies of your half-time buddies hang half-hanged in Smithfield, I'm lounging on a swivel chair in a law firm's wood-lined corner-office, stinking of leather, flicking through lists of big wigs (literally), artists' catalogues, the poetry of exile (yours).

You're my man, he said, but the squeal of the lift couldn't mask the mark of the market.

To help protect your privacy, the trauma of the gaping throng blocking the way at Giltspur Street, a hood of sack-cloth or a faceful of ash will suffice to hide your visage.

Turns out this fear of earth's endemic, Will.

The rocks of which you speak; the endless sea at night like a huge black pall thrown from a different gaoler's fist.

This prison is an island.

But who's the slave, Will?
And who, the god?

Sent: 6 January 2009 21:10
To: William Dodd <wdodd@hammers.com>;
Subject: speculate to accumulate

Treat this as fan mail, or whatever. We both know it's more
complex than we would like. I know not how to leave / break
off, I tell thee; only add to your mixed bag of fan, hate mail,
spam and worthy parish circulars.

I snared the gaping crowd, Will; told Akerman you once
danc'd into the living grave wherein we're food for worms.
I'd love to see your homely porter, clad in bespoke skin of
wolsey grey; strange choirs, guttural outpourings.

I'm what you'd call a fellow traveller; terrestrial stranger
with my twin-pack scriptures, ghostly doctrine tagged along
the walls. Watch for the pattern and the source, you said.

The pattern: infamy!
The source: infamy!

There is no other word for this. All must be real, my friend;
all must be real. I give thee Newgate: welcome to the end
of speculation.

Sent: 7 September 2008 15:58
To: Jack Shepherd
Subject: Howdunnit?

Having studied all the diagrams in the broadsheets (where H denotes a chimney flume and J – well, you get the picture) I would like, dear Jack, to make an alternate proposal; that like the Ripper and your Springheeled namesake *you* were never there. Trompe l'oeil, Jack. A false wall put up to hide the view. Jack watching Jack watching us. If I looked you up now, I'd find you flogging faulty flatscreens off Tottenham Court Road, or down in Spitalfields, hustling the hipsters in a deep Scottish brogue, feet bound in newsprint.

I must split: the new run of *Prison Break*'s on and anyway, I'm sure that this will bounce.

Eyes right; but you're pointing off left.

Immortality's a pamphlet away.
This makes me – the competition.

MYRA CONNELL

PENINSULA

Pen-
insula.

Thrust
out

precar-
ious.

Peninsular,
an almost island.

Almost-island
woman

penis-woman,
thrust out

for-
saken.

I have seen
your eyes,

your nape,
your

anxious neck.

EARLSWOOD GARDEN CENTRE CAFÉ

Came out the door, turned right instead of left.
The rain will start. Black clouds are coming over.
There's a raw place in the gut. A second cord is breaking
and I can't find South.
People come to choose their gravel, don't see me.
The list's a token. List's a bulwark, lifebelt:
joke. Two firs, and two perhaps of sycamore or elm,
two halves, together, like the houses of a heart. I'm quiet
in my corner, here behind the fence. Men are speaking
weights of topsoil, half a metre cubed, and decking,
white like sunshine. The brightness in the sky is
not enough for shadows and
I can't find South.

From the Valley

From the valley, trees seemed frosted.
Up close, each twig a ghost, a shadow made of ice,
each twig, all along the ridge
and pushing in to sparse bare woods.

And did I say? About the pool?
He took my hand, said, *Here.*
This way, and led me round the back,
behind the crumbling wall –

an awkward turn, a stepping stone –
(the smell of frying eggs, stale smoke)
and there, a deep black pool.
Carp moved goldly,

muscled. Go today. See carp.
Go anywhere with walls, deep pools,
and gold (but don't say gold)
leaves floating

cold.

Horse sale

It's a bolter, that's for sure. Takes fright it does, and yes,
they tried to sell it. Paraded it, that's led it by a halter;
ran beside it, in the auction ring, the man's coat flapping, 's if
    it was
prime stock. It wasn't. There was the shaggy coat for starters,
fuzzing off its belly like a half-done moult, a dried-up yellow.
Then the thin neck, hanging, and the long and flaccid dick,
more a bag than instrument. A broken horse, sway-backed,
teetering on ballerina toes.

                     Who'd buy that? Not me.
No, never, not a chance. If nothing else, the feet would put
    me off.
Never seen a horse with such small feet. No-one had,
or seemed to know for sure:
but thought he'd be unstable. Old and broken-winded,
and this coarse old body and the feet so neat.

No chance.

PRAYER

(Gloria Jean's, Friday, late November)

I hadn't known how cold it was.
Sun here, on this spot, and
quiet voices;

the man, from somewhere, playing the accordion,
keeping foot-time with a tambourine.
Sun,

last leaves,
the quiet shadow. Tacky
gap-tooth car-park,

paintbrush trees, and distance.
I have my beetroot in the bag for salad
(pears, blue cheese);

have cabbage, January King,
and Cara bakers. There's
the sound of the accordion;

that bobbed and belted woman;
smell of toasting cheese; barristas
holding party court and flirting;

pigeons, one one-footed, draggled;
and the shadow of the church.

Let me not lose this yet.

CLAIRE CROWTHER

MOLLICLE

'I'll take the baby
when it's born.'
The strange god landed
in my bed,
naked. His offer
frightened me.
I must keep
my mollicle.   *daughter*

I said: 'Give up
the other. Better,
I'll love you
unconditionally.'
A skin of need
agrees conditions
when you have
a mollicle

but appeasement
never ends.
How I hated
his winged ankles.
To save my only
mollicle
I found a bar
of steel to ram

up my backbone.
Steel of courage
close up brittles,
not worth ramming.
Still, I kept my
mollicle
till she took
herself away.

Ash-heart

Had I not had a previous name,
a little grave to take plants to,

I wouldn't have stopped by that stone,
or thought to see the woman I was

before the sack of home: young
self, silent, breathing styles

of sound – not words, the robber fog
that flows around recognition.

Gout weed covers her library
but I flush her with my language:

'Grass knits bodies, knits roots.
Speechless archivist, when sun-

incinerated moon grits
our view, then, my ash-heart,

day and night, repay your loan:
shine with sun's compulsive light.'

THE ALICES

I said he was brillig and I meant it.
He stood in the hall of a friend's house
offering extra as simply as a hostess
carrying crockery, the only one of us

who has actually fought the jabberwock,
whose face we see on *News at Ten*,
whose name is called at tribunals, who defies
James Naughtie on *Today*. He talked

about mome raths, saying hesitantly,
'If the raths don't outgrabe.'
I loathed seeing him like that, stooping
below somebody's lintel, being slithy.

'It's not about gyring,' he snapped.
But it was. Later he told me how
after a tough meeting, in the distance
he'd seen me climbing out of a car,

my body suggesting something else to save.
The houses our set restored fetched fortunes.
Was that better behaviour? A brillig affair!
So special a person to have taken to wabe.

I thought, they all do it, the toves.
The tension, the criticism they get
for neglecting their children, the fear
of borogoves. We support them,

us Alices. But we're mome. 'To me
you could never be mome,' he said,
'whatever you decide' as he left.

HERITAGE

'*Get That Tiger* isn't a hymn,' my mother
muttered under the muttering of the Mass.

Later, her Costa face tint showed up odd
against the plain Tudor Catholic walls.

The priests' hole behind a bookshelf was labelled
a library. 'Can't have had much learning,'

a blonde boy said. 'Douai,' said Father Thomas.
I scrambled down a ladder. At the bottom, soil.

'Not much they'd be doing here,' said Phyllis,
'but praying.' It isn't a hymn. Monks were dressed

as celebrities. We photographed them, laughing
by the moat. 'They dress up for visitors,'

Big Nurnie said. 'Cassocks.' My mother slapped
her sandwich down on her missal. My son kept on

about the ways they executed priests.
'Who is this *they*?' I asked. It isn't a hymn.

There comes a time when you switch off from listening
and lose someone. I traced her back to the hole.

O Mary, Mother of God, you get that tiger,
full of grace, and you sing her to us.

WHERE ARE YOU GOING?

I usually say 'Home'.
Today I say 'Europe to Europe'.

The border guard pulls me over,
takes my passport, leaves.

Crags rank over the Rhône.
A hood of cloud blinds Mont Blanc.

After an hour, he throws
my passport through my window.

I don't drive off. I smear
the head of a block of unsalted

on a crust of bread.
I chew each mouthful thirty-five times.

He bangs on the car roof. 'Butter?
Too much and we'll confiscate it.

You know the rules.' I grind
my gold bars underfoot.

ANGELA FRANCE

PROSPECT

Peer into hedgerows,
part thickets and look
in their dark centres,
trail through pine woods,
kick through leaves under beech trees.
    Clear the ditches,
drag the pond, examine each tangle
of weed and scrap of metal,
use a pole to prod deep
until you know there's nothing there.
    Check the outhouses;
move the old bikes, the mower,
the paint cans and scraps of wood.
Rake through the dusty nuggets
of coal in the corner, pull cobwebs
away from the shelves, ignore
gritty smears on your hands.
    Go home. Search the cellar,
the attic, pull out boxes from under beds,
chests from closets. Look inside.
Learn to wait.

GETTING HERE FROM THERE

I name where I tread
grass, rock, mud
to fix the ground beneath me.

A door ajar.
Inside, a smell of emptiness,
a taste of waiting; logs stacked
by the grate, blankets folded on a bed.

On the mantelpiece, a cracked mirror
and a bottle holding a curl of dark hair.
A book lies on the table, my name
on the cover, its pages blank.
The wall opposite the window
has nails knocked into a beam
to hold a large map
                                    of my skin.

I stay the day, studying the map.
                    And I stay the days after,
learning the setting of each mole
and freckle, rebuilding
an inch at a time.

When the hair in the bottle is streaked
with grey, I wash and fold blankets,
sweep the grate, chop logs to stack.
I take down the map, roll it
to fit my backpack, pocket the bottle,
leave the door ajar.

Canzone: Cunning

My marrow is veined with cunning;
history is written in our bones.
Not sneaky, like a fox, sort of cunning
nor a neat design sort of cunning;
not an adjective, but a title given
or grown into. A different cunning
which forms in the gut; a cunning
earning a capital over hard-worn time.
A woman, or man, doesn't count time
until someone calls *Hey, Cunning!*
It's not me they call but an old woman
who runs in my veins, a cunning woman.

You always knew what you were, old woman.
I grew knowing the wink of your cunning,
the cackle and knock of a comfortable woman
who had aged past appearances. Oh, woman,
your grin seeded such an itch in my bones
to plant my feet on dark earth, to be a woman
who lives in her own skin, a woman
who pricks importance with profanity. It's given
a sense of the lightness that held you, given
me the weight of what it means to be woman,
to skate before the pressure-wave of passing time,
to harvest and hoard the gathering marks of time.

When everything was beginning, time
was a kaleidoscope. Becoming a woman
seemed just out of reach, fragments of time
spun away by wishing. Naïve of the tricks time
plays, it took years to match it in cunning;
stretching when I wanted it to shrink, time
raced on when I wanted to hold it still. Time
teases with knowledge growing as bones
weaken; by the time I felt in my bones
who and where I needed to be, time
had already taken more of the years given
than there were years left still to be given.

It's too easy to forget what we're given
by old women over the cradle, betting against time.
But I recall the nudge, wink, and grin I was given
when you won at cards or your steady look, given
to me when you saw shade over a man, or woman,
and knew they'd come to the end of the time given.
You never told what you'd given,
left in trust to mature into cunning.
Before I could name it, I knew your cunning
had come to me; knew something had been given,
passed down. I knew it in the grinding of my bones
but had no word for it until it had worn my bones

to creaking. There's little spring left in my bones,
lines map my skin to trace all I've given
and I feel my flesh hang heavy on my bones.
In the mirror, I see you in the shape of my bones,
in the length of my nose, in the weight time
leaves on me. I hear the rattle of your bones
and feel you chuckle when I see you in my bones;
when I was young, you were always old, woman,
but I'm where you were and don't feel an old woman.
Years slip through my fingers, gravity drags at bones;
I don't fear getting old if it comes with your cunning;
your shape, your heft, your cunning.

Not an adjective, not sneaky-like-a-fox cunning;
but the cunning in the sight of a comfortable woman
who has accepted her indenture to time,
who has lifted the lid on what was long given,
who knows what quickens in the marrow of our bones.

WHAT IS HIDDEN

So many small lives, pushing through
soil below our feet; cogs within
clocks; wintering bees; the black skin
of polar bears; the missing screw;
the way I still feel about you.
How swifts live a whole life in flight;
the words in a book when the light
is out; squirrels' hoards; the odd sock;
the sculpture in a rough wood block;
what terrors wake me through the night.

CUNNING

The potatoes planted on a new moon. New shoes
never on the table. The colour green kept from the house.

A coat never laid on a bed. White lilac held separate
from mauve. The luck that shouldn't be named.

The handshake away from the table. The china horses
turned from the door. The broom never leant on a bed.

Fingernail clippings always thrown on the fire. Breath held
at the cemetery gate. The doors unlocked for a death.

The trick on the doorstep. Pepper under a pillow.
The cards that always turn up in time.

An unseen gesture. The string on the banister.
Ashes in the graveyard. The wink at church carvings.

> The wind you can't stop from blowing,
> how you say it always sobs your name.

OTHER TONGUES

When I say I'm alone, I'm lying.
My mother tongue sleeps under my skin,
bred in the bone, colouring my blood.
I speak from an echo chamber
where the walls pulse with whispers,
familiar cadences rising and falling
at my back. I speak from a limestone floor,
as familiar to my feet as are the bones
of the hill creaking between the roots
of great beeches. I speak with multitudes
in my throat, their round vowels
vibrating in my stomach, their pitch
and tone stiffening my spine.

ANDREW FROLISH

CONSTRUCTION

All the forces collide in him,
the electro-magnet, the compound heart,
the crucible of manufacturing.
In the blackened whorls of his fingers
are a thousand stains of invention,
blood-spilled remains of oily assembly,
the carved metal of miners' lamps and stamps
of codes and places on his products —
the physical proof of his passing through.
In his hands, my father inspects the shining skin
of a new lamp, testing the spark as he forces the flint.

Beneath his overalls and grease and grime,
he is distinguished by a starched collar and tie.
Now see him, in this windowless place,
hand resting tenderly on a metal plate,
encouraging its hum, its tick, its work rate
with a carefully forged whisper, and they breathe
together, like one great machine, stronger
than the sum of my parts; they mould, make, measure.

In the artificial light, no one sees the cloud rise,
an invisible fog of chemical bile.
And yet he knows it; senses a shift in the atoms
and an interference in the cogs and whirs of creation.
This is a drama of working men. Evacuation.
While we make our way outside, blinded
by handfuls of summer light, he remains
to engineer a healing process, hands on.

Outside, I bask alone in the warmth of a summer
we had forgotten; formed in our absence.
My father follows the piston-punching siren call
while workers wait in the shadow of the factory wall.

And this is how the myth of factory hero
is pieced together, a construction in time
of memorised tools, cogs, pumps and grime;
hands crafting over fists pummelling, a life
spent manufacturing this man; the myth is mine.

TRANSIENT WORKER

The way he used to lean on the machine,
bare elbow on its hot, metal skin —
I always felt that when he went away,
he would leave something of himself behind.
Local radio was neglected
while we listened to his mixtapes,
singing along in the factory din.
And when they told him to get on
with his work, sometimes he did.

At the next machine, I wore gloves
to handle the hot tools
and to purge the near-liquid plastic
but his hands would rest
on the humming metal, not melting
or blistering, and still they were
the hands and fingers of a pianist.

One day he didn't show. And the next.
I kept expecting him to swagger in,
a grin, a nod and an unlikely story.
We made do, filled in, started on time
and queued to clock out in an orderly fashion.
After a week we tuned the radio back in.

REMNANTS

Briefly, like the last wave
before the next, he imagines
removing his clothing, layer by layer,
morning by evening, beginning by end,
and leaving each item folded neatly
in a small pile of unnecessary names,
and walking out into the restless murk.

Almost invisible from the shore now,
a smudge against the heaving wash,
he could slide down amongst half-remembered
snippets of sound and vision,
leaving no letter to inform us of our loss:
just a small pile of tidy remnants

for those who still believe
in second chances.

THE LAST TO KNOW

Perhaps I can't quite see it,
as if your hand is curled around it,
a guilty little secret on a crumpled note.
It is something that you fold up
and slip away, hoping I don't see
but half-hoping that I do.
Under the tables, it goes
from hand to hand, lap to lap,
until everyone but me has seen it
and covertly passed it back.

I'm the sort who thinks the worse
if the option is presented;
the kind who worries first
before settling into panic.
When you conceal the only things
that I want to know,
you force me to take your hand
and prise the slender fingers apart:
because in your hand,
I think you hold your heart.

ROZ GODDARD

I Want To Be An Angel

I give you this, a silver coin.
Keep it in your pocket
and know by touching it
you cannot be bad.
When you are sockless, without a coat,
when your mother is drunk asleep in the afternoon,
heavy curtains keeping out the sun,
when your father creases the living room door –
touch the coin.
When you are left at school with the cleaners
when you count stars on the long walk home
when you pray for silence;
land in your seventh town
with its unfamiliar trams and roofs of northern rain,
touch the coin.
Remember what I said
that soft crayon-smelling afternoon
the two of us bent over the extraordinary words
you had written.
Remember what I told you.

HOME, 1974

Thank you Ted Heath, for the Three Day Week,
for the cluster of us in the darkened room,

for the necks of candles shell pink, their flames
bowing in the heat of our collected voices.

We abandoned chill rooms for the back kitchen,
how comical it was and how perfect;

for a few weeks only we laughed in the stalls
of our own family play – 'look at dad's nose

on the wall, it's enormous.' Seams of coal
slept on, as we gorged on delight and couldn't move.

A holiday from gravity had presented itself,
and in those evenings we were fabulous in our relaxation.

There was no need of the August sea, the soft rage
of it folding sequins of sun in on itself,

no appetite for the sparking dodgems
or the noisy pier where we had walked

in silence wondering where the fun was.
Here we were with a few flames, a few thrown

shadows, and outside the rubbish stacked
the walls like sandbags, holding back the flood.

from THE SOPRANOS SONNETS

Christopher

Oh, Christopher, believe me, I'm with you;
it's hard being ordinary, with a surfeit
of feeling that won't elegantly form itself.
Inadequacy of thought, of sensibility,
is a grave handicap in this writing life
we have chosen. Every day the same:
stumbling in the alleys looking for a gift
out of there, lost again in a dark city.

I understand why you chose killing –
it can be done like fixing up a shelf.
There was a tendency in you to stand
back and admire your deft handiwork.
Like the bodies were stories in long grass –
that first unbelievable paragraph.

Dr. Melfi

She is untangling him still, taking out snakes
one by one, turning their bodies in the light,
pointing out the silver and purple
iridescence of their skins, saying, *'Look Tony,*
see how they twist?' *'See how they're all trying*
to get somewhere?' He pays her to make
him thoughtful, to ease him through dark water,
she has no absolution to offer.

He thinks science beautiful, all that learning
captured like so many butterflies in her
fabulous head. He's distracted by the hem
of her skirt, the hinterland between New
Jersey and paradise. Could he take her today?
Her words are surely blown kisses, foreplay.

Adriana

Sil is still Tony's dark, untethered dog,
sniffing at the gate, cocking an ear
for hints of war. Chris's gloom is towering,
and Johnny Sack? He's mad for his own wife.
New Jersey is grey, the sun out-done by
canopies and SUV's, Vito's stare.
Adriana died, taken out hard
on a long Tuesday full of sky and rain.

Back in my own still life, in soft autumn sun
between the weeding and accepting post,
I couldn't shake her gold curls, long french nails,
her out-of-placeness in the woods, her plea.
Lines of words are slackened telegraph wires
the guns stay quiet, red leaves mimic fire.

DAVID HART

from THE TITANIC CAFÉ CLOSES ITS DOORS AND HITS THE ROCKS

What is to be waste
and what to be kept,
what to cancel out
and what to treasure?
What is our wellness
and what is our sickness?

Where we live,
where we are,
where we be
in the city diddly dee.

Lost in wonder, love and that was then,
alone in chorus to scavenge heaven
for poppies there more bright than ours
sprouted from blood and sweat and tears
for heart's ease and scavenge
in the hope so to arrange
and be arranged for readiness
beyond the wharf and cut –

The theatre of THE BEST TEA IN THE UK
            is falling down,
the canal isn't deep enough for the TITANIC CAFÉ
to sink without trace, there'd be a fine mess.
            All but ready to collapse
            of its own volition. Listen,
a child on a longboat along from Bournville asks,

What's that?! 'It's a
planks and struts and frames by numbers temple
  to the God of Advertising
where you could buy God's Own Tea
till the God of Storm
    took it away almost.'
Birds Foot Trefoil - Eggs & Bacon, Ham
& Eggs, Hen & Chickens, Tom Thumb, Lady's Slipper,
Granny's Toenails, Fingers & Thumbs, Cuckoo's Stockings,
Dutchman's Clogs – a place exquisitely lit
by eyes that know it.
    Ah to escape all shit,
by day and night
and be disembodied thought.

 Stop at the lights,
 move at the lights.

Everything can go into little bags,
Sainsbury's old and new can go into a little bag,
what remains of the Battery Co. can go into one,
the new hospital can go into one with the university,
the Worcester & Birmingham canal can be drained
    into a purse
and the concrete can be folded into a handkerchief,
the Knife & Fork Café as was can go into a black bag,
the whole wild flower *waste ground* can go into one,
Selly Oak library can go into a little glo-bag,
a little polythene bag will be plenty for the Bristol Road,
another for COMET, B&Q, HOMEBASE and the rest,
another bag for the Dingle,
all of them in a trail of little bags,
a little bag now for the railway station and a Cross City

and a Virgin Pendolino that happens to be crossing,
a little bag for all the people in Selly Oak at 3 a.m.
            this Easter Sunday,
all the dogs in a little bag, all the cats in another,
all the cars, vans, lorries, motorbikes and buses
            in a crisp packet,
            for Christmas.

Light
has been located from what was out there in nowhere
3.3 billion years ago, travelling for all that time from
        near the beginning of the universe
        reckoned at 13.7 billion years
    'when those stars were beginning to form'.

    I wear red socks in bed,
    they encourage the flow of blood.
    In snug night air
    I am rushing nowhere, then

    the towpath's a throughway,
    an old kind of throughway,
    the tunnels are tricky
    but tricky is normal, and

    red socks in bed
            encourage the blood.

It's not a hut, it's not, it's not,
and yet there is a huttishness about it,
    from which urgencies:
as Holderlin from his yellow tower,
Kafka from his corridor,

Heidegger from his hut in the wood,
like Basho whose name was hut, and
not like any of them at all.

     But yes like, so like!

Mallow – Bread & Cheese,
Pick-cheeses – exquisitely lit,
but don't eat, don't eat.

Can I leave my card?
 Stick it on the board.
LOOKING FOR A QUIET HOLIDAY IN THE SUN?
 With the others, getting a bit dog-eared:
COMPRESSOR SERVICES
    GLASS AND GLAZING
  AUTO-ELECTRICS
    SECURITY SERVICES
  VALETING
ELECTRICAL
   ROOFING
      They were here?
   Oh yes.
With their little cards?
 Put their heads round the door, that's all, some of 'em,
 some stayed for egg and chips, don't know that
 anyone ever reads 'em. Anyway, you're welcome.
Egg and chips then. And beans. And tea. Please.
 Push the boat out, have bacon.
Boat's out then, bacon. And sausage.
 And two sugars in the tea?
 Made my day.
You're welcome.

Out the back in the deep of grass and flowers,
phosphorous and God knows what not safe
for a stoat after a snipe's eggs if there's a snipe,
if there's a stoat, a vole getting it in the neck
if there are voles, if there are stoats, a rabbit if
there are rabbits sniffing lavender – there *is*
lavender – if there is a watch worth the trouble
for a sparrow hawk, if the fox doesn't bother to
lurk beyond from the park, no matter,
no heron, teal or coot straying from the Rea,
            no matter

            all to go under, to go under
            as the planet turns and burns,
            all to go under, to go under: these:

Moon Daisy - Ox-Eye Daisy, Moon Penny, Field Daisy,
Dog Daisy, Marguerite; Lady's Smock - Cuckoo Flower,
Milkmaids, Fairy Flower, May Flower, Birds Foot Trefoil
- Eggs & Bacon, Ham & Eggs, Hen & Chickens, Tom
Thumb, Lady's Slipper, Granny's Toenails, Fingers &
Thumbs, Cuckoo's Stockings, Dutchman's Clogs; Mallow
- Bread & Cheese, Pick-cheeses; Black Knapweed, Self
Heal, Lady's Bedstraw, Black Medic, Red Clover,
Ox-eye Daisy, Yarrow, Knapweed, Chickweed, Mallow,
Sorrel, Betony, Foxglove, Meadowsweet, Teasel, more
Meadowsweet, Poppy, Harebell, Sun Spurge, Common
Fumitory, Creeping Thistle, Knapweed, Evening
Primrose, Bugle, Forget Me Not, Poppy, all exquisitely
lit, exquisitelylit and cared about like shit. Bulldoze
those bastard flowers
        reminding us.
            Bulldoze 'em!

The mask is laid aside
and the mask is slid on again
and laid aside
and now is clamped on
because the sudden light in the night
seems to show
and to obscure,
to reveal from beginning to end,
and to deny with neither word
nor no-word. This is us,
wave, go on, wave.

Under here somewhere –
oh if I could dowse in Welsh –
comes Birmingham's water,
the Elan aqueduct's constancy –
the A-Z shows it plainly –
from that lovely valley,
(I've been there, so near, so far,
and to Cannon Hill Park's tiny replica).
Has there been a re-route
because of the new road?
Can the Lazy Fox be located
as a co-ordinate?

Empty is open to another good meal
                somewhere
        to more empty to more
                somewhere
        good food or bad
and more empty and to sing then,
        oh yes to sing

that it's a laughing and crying matter
        being here
leaving melancholic traces to be collected
in one of God's Senior Officers' plastic bags
        ready for
heaven's forensics. The clouds
have news for us, want to tell us their news,
want to rain so sodding hard on bread
that has sustained us from real wheat
in real fields, and to rain sodding hard
        on the poems
of bystanders. If you're into a sandwich
and reading this poem, the clouds say,
get yourself a boat, a good strong boat.

        The skin evacuates.

The melancholy of the interface sucks in
flowers and crushes them. Binky boo boo.
        All those tin whistles.

So we walked all night during the afternoon
looking for the animal with no name or skin
        amongst the flowers that had no stem.

Soul boopy boopy needs skill
    to feel this kind of unwell
   in the face of the delusion
      that all is well.

Gone now, the Knife and Fork Titanic
without the dignity of sinking even

in shallow water, but knocked down
and taken away
in a lorry.
The new Sainsbury's will sell hot tea
so that's OK.

Poet's note: *A cleared space now, in Selly Oak, Birmingham, where the canal goes under the Bristol (originally Roman) Road and where the railway goes over it, is where there had once been a substantial shack of a building, the welcoming Titanic Café. The café took a hit from high winds and, over the months of mid-2007, demolition men did the rest. I spent much of that time hanging around the area, where a huge new Sainsbury's was planned and (in the downturn) not built, while in scrubland beside the canal wild flowers were prolific. I found background on the web and from elsewhere and what is a fractured and I hope celebratory long poem came to be. The extract from that poem here runs from mid-way to the end. There is a YouTube film about the poem and the cafe, with a wander around the area after the demolition, and photographs, at:*
http://www.youtube.com/watch?v=zIYVxoh3Xo0

LUKE KENNARD

Oh, You Don't Agree?

I don't want to sound like a prophet,
but last night I found over twenty things in Revelation
that could be metaphors for the internet.

I'm going to pretend I overheard that in *Pret A Manger*;
a pretty young mother said it to her baby son.
She ate a beef and watercress sandwich.

She said many beautiful and terrible things.
The smile of the ducks on his pram was beautiful
and terrible. All children are psychic.

I'm drinking this new red coffee, but then I swallow,
hard. There is no red coffee. It doesn't exist.
Her long black coat is a tundra in profile. She turns

on me like a security camera. She offers her hand.
'I'm Miranda,' she says. 'This is Simon.'
'You're going to be hearing a lot about yourself on the radio.

We're here to make sure it's all great!'
House like a dozen bookshelves fished out of a canal.
House like a stranger's Christmas. The baby says,

'It's always sad in the alcoholic wing
when they wake up screaming,
"I saw Hell in a tomato! I saw Hell in a tomato!"'

I too have seen Hell in a tomato.

101 STATE-SANCTIONED PRACTICAL JOKES

Today they carpeted the inside of my piano.
It sounds like an old couple kicking over a jumble sale.

I bite into a tomato and when I look at it
it looks exactly like the mouth which bit it.

'Don't play with your tomato,' says Simon.
I laugh. The activist is being interviewed.

A writer or a fishstick, says the radio, *it's up to you.*
I have always hated the activist, but now I don't know.

Maybe you can't drive around in 'Being Really Well Read',
honking at pretty girls as they totter between clubs;

maybe you can't admire the muscle definition
of intellectual rigour in a full-length mirror, but...

We are starting to see the activist's point:
that we, too, are cowards and bullies.

When the activist gets home he climbs
into a sachet of preserving agent.

When the activist shoots us in the stomach
we curl around the bullets like cats.

'MORE SAD NEWS FROM YOUR STUPID PLANET'

I make a cup of tea for each of the 68 cups in the house.
Given that matter cannot be created or destroyed,
some of these cups must contain fragments of asteroid
from before the world began, which is amazing.

I arrange the cups of tea all over the ground floor.
The door knocks over two. 'Hi Simon. Cup of tea?'
He's getting good; barely flinches. Picks up a cup.
Takes a sip. Sighs. 'You may be batshit crazy,

but you certainly make a good cup of tea.'
Between us we drink every single cup. I am beginning
to like Simon, his courteous smile like a weak
line-break, the fashionable cut of his jaw-line.

Miranda is out on the Vespa delivering death threats.
"This is just more sad news from your stupid planet."
She is the most private, ecstatic, non-confrontational
person I have ever met. She owns several parasols.

Everything has been so, so wonderful today
I think I will drink some poison and not be killed by it,
but then it's back to the A&E for grim smiles, clipboards,
ammonia smell, green walls, machines.

'Trouble is,' I explain to Simon before they ask me to count to ten,
'I'm so insecure I can't stand to hear anyone else complimented.
Even for something in which I have no interest.
If you said, *Herman is the best mountain climber I've ever met,*

I'd secretly resent Herman. *So what am I? Chopped liver?*
Am I some chopped liver trying to climb a mountain?
Flubbing onto the snowy rocks and partially freezing
on the underside? Picked at by huskies? Mountain doves?

But then I apologise for sounding all weird.
I am worried that Simon might be fired
because I drank the poison on his watch,
so I call my notary public and have him witness

the following statement at my bedside:
'I didn't drink the poison because I was sad:
I drank it because I was too happy.'
And he writes it down, verbatim:

I DIDN'T DRINK THE POISON BECAUSE I WAS SAD:
I DRANK IT BECAUSE I WAS TOO HAPPY.
'Maybe an exclamation mark,' I murmur.
He disagrees. 'Where's Miranda?' I ask.

'She practically *is* an exclamation mark;
She'd understand. One... Two... Three... Four...'
Unconsciousness like an apple falling into a bowl of soup.
An apple thrown out of a mirror and caught, off-screen.

TRUE STORY OF MY OWN DEATH #2

"Incident Report: patient has now returned to the Home,
wiser and perhaps a little sadder."

Simon fills in a B86 Incident Report form.
He files it in a cabinet marked B86 Incident Reports.

Miranda is rubbing peppermint foot lotion onto my feet.
'Your poor feet,' she says.

Today a consultant is visiting. He arrives in a black Jaguar:
the kind of car a consultant *should* drive.

'It's like jelly, see,' he says, holding before me
a big tray bearing an oblong green jelly,

a perceptible shadow in one end.
'We cut out the bad bit...'

Here the doctor produces a kitchen knife,
slices away the shadowy quarter of the jelly,

'...and throw it away,' he says.
He scrapes the shadowy jelly into the bin.

Then he scrapes the good jelly into the bin,
having illustrated the point.

'You must get through a lot of jelly,' I say, cheerfully.
The doctor laughs. 'We certainly do.'

Why am I so kind to doctors?
A stubby cloud is hanging in the sky so low I laugh at it.

'No more twilit stupor hearing the spanner clang on the
　　radiators,'
I sing. 'No more coffee-mud and boredom-frigid air.'

Boat sounds, plaintive then resigned. The necropolis boat:
funny to see my face in every porthole, grinning,

funny and perhaps also not funny at all.

FIN

A kitten will fight its own reflection,
but stop abruptly around its first birthday.
Up until now I believed that was because the cat
had come to understand what a mirror was,
but that now strikes me as crazy.
Cats can't even understand gravity,
let alone mirrors. So it is more the case
that the cat knows not to mess
anymore with the glass cat
who uncannily blocks its every attack.

MILORAD KRYSTANOVICH

OUT OF DARKROOMS

The lady and the castle-builder
walk along the beach,
a camera hanging around her neck,
his shadow slipping away.

Are you listening to me?
Taking the photograph of a trough,
she cannot hear her own voice
or his reply – *yes, if you are the sea.*

Wave after wave feeds the moats
around the sand castles,
the breeze creeping upon her hair
but not blowing it across the lens.

Are you following the boat?
He paddles in the shallows
and cannot hear himself or her response –
yes, if its sail matches my skirt.

The summer air laces to its frame
in the picture of the low sky:
coping with the sound of water,
the afternoon is their only burden.

Presence

When it was time, you held your doll
and sat on your dad's shoulders
under his umbrella, under that shade of dark.

As he walked through the rain's perpetual tune
chancing your childhood, brightening the grey,
you hummed how the raindrops drummed the black cloth:

tap-tap, tap-tap, the rainwater was fragmented
into separate tones, each drop a note in music,
you closed your ears half on yourself, half on your voice.

it conjured the rhythm of your flight
among the people in the street and you wished
no ending, no landing, no being alone.

Now it's raining again and you feel the sky
could stay over the clouds forever:
harmony expands her hold on daylight

and the day is spread out by its form
while her lover's hand on her shoulder
rejuvenates the membrane of her smile.

Tap-tap, tap-tap, the rainfall cannot reach her
under the transparent bell of her umbrella:
the drummer on her way to the shrine of melody,

she hears the passers-by praising
one who has directed the rainwater concert –
the composer returns to the certainty of her song.

Late Honeymoon

The fire eats a book of poetry.
Their meal will be served
just before the cold ashes
pile themselves in the fire-place.

Dancing with two armfuls of sea-water
they leave the late evening,
their footprints lead them
from the kaleidoscope
of memory to the house of reality.

Their footsteps guide them to the end
of their honeymoon dance:
nothing can go backwards
apart from the midwinter.

Moonlight follows them
and passes through the door
they have not closed,
their shadows absorb
the warm air of the tourist resort.

Dream Gap

Night streams through the midsummer
and darkens the fenced enclosure.
Not irritated by the lime tree blossom,
they sleep near the pine tree.

Coloured like the skin of the moon,
the garden is no longer their property,
not even they can tame the sky to enter
and mend their entwined dream.

Clothed only in tree flowers,
passers-by sing and dance in their clogs,
none of them halt to wake the sleepers
to listen to their steps and their song:

we cannot fall asleep and join you
in the base of dying moonlight,
not even our shadows leave
our outstretched arms,
nor can we change
this serenade into
an empty silence.

RORSCHACH TEST

Your writing is made up of music
with a blank dot at the end of the stave,
you play your fountain-pen – your flute
releases the air in the pattern of sound
while you reveal what a mountain can reach,

touching the inky sky: *Take my breath –*
your compass for the untitled evening concert –
and dance with your fingers across the flute.
Each fingertip in its place, each can search
for the coordinates of a classical minuet.

As if a butterfly is flying to the florists
and leads me to find a spray of roses for you –
a musician bowing from the symphony stage,
I hold the butterfly wings – the essence
of a metaphor fading in the palm of my hand,

exposed to the street lamp: *Go back to the garden*
where you cut the flowers from their green cradles
and let the butterfly follow you on your return
to the meadow where a still life never does exist
and listen to the major keys of the vacuum.

If this test is folded in half and laid on the stand,
the image is divided into the silence that counts –
the interval between the past and the future,
echoing the poem from the paper,
the act of prevailing.

RUTH LARBEY

FUNGLISH

in beaks, in coats, on the air,
the spores of funglish
broadcast a persistent contagion,
a black-market pestilence –
the beginnings of our sentences   die in the middle

we hatched out those poisons
that stunk in the mud,
scratched our dreams into songs,
blind in the dust –

unseeming, unstitching –

whilst a post-mortem shock registers:
we knew none of the secrets
coming out of our mouths
and still don't

we stole those words
that congealed with meaning,

(bubbled heavily)
went bad on the inside –

sick; rank and wicked,
our mouths mildewed and wanting,

with the spores of a funglish that's

hard to
define

THE NORTHERN LINE

My friend said he once saw four eyes around a candle

between Monument and London Bridge,

as the steampunked cars huffed and clunked,

creaked, *shunted*, through the Victorian pitch.

Four eyes in the flickering damp; *different*,

I'm sure, to the pointless frisson of mutual gaze

when, for seconds, your lit-up train marries another in the gloom.

Here, recession sucks air from the vacuum tube, pre-transistor.

That's an unforgiving jolt, the voltage of shock from four eyes

between Monument and London Bridge.

It forced a gasp of stifled breath

from a diaphragm (compressed);

a protest, at this '**Crisis of the West!**'

Our buzzing hive, and its heedless rise,

behoves us to test this old imagined entity;

behoves us to be the progenitories

of a different power, a different story: heterodyne.

Those eyes underground flash past into present,

where, in the air above our heads, devious metaphors

dog-fight; sell things; sell lives; sell

more discounted ways to get away from what we've got.

If you listen well you'll be able to hear:

dot-dot-dot-dash-dash-dash-dot-dot-dot.

Subtle S.O.S. above the daily stress; hushed,

suppressed, lest it drowns the drones of so many iPods.

Something Moved

He smiled from inside the metal door.
I'll see you at home he said, and
didn't kiss me.

Listening carefully one day
something moved
and I felt hot with the first surge of what
it felt like to live branchlessly.

Now, whenever the day brightens
suddenly, like a tin-foil-flash,

I know the world is dark elsewhere.

QUESTION

We ask: were our past masters deceived?
Did our parents believe in the things they were told?
That beggar-your-neighbour was old and sage?
Remember where this started? In someone else's dream –

and the first impression
still remains to be seen.

To believe in one poorly spun, perforated
story of change over another just the same;
is it a careful spray on pampered skin,
when what we need is rain?

A drenching to the core of our
well-worn lines upon the floor...?

CHRIS McCABE

BLOOMSBURY

for Kelvin Corcoran

It's the music of what *matters*
it pulls me this way always
across Waterloo Bridge
in search of the poet
— revenant of sliproad hymns —
the Isle of Dogs smatters
its SIM cards to the stars
as Westminster descales
gold florins
in the Counting House
of the river's pummelling,
the Aldwych arcs a scythe against
Bush House & pushes me north
— in search of the poet —
through the contented Squares
of Tavistock, Russell, Bloomsbury,
where my mind lost its trace —
night air around Gt. Ormond St
when my son was strung with fluids
like a doll in a rockpool
I walk that way through reduced serotonin
to the glyphs of SWEDENBORG HALL
inside the poet sings
with a haemorrhage on his mind —
adds his message to the city's signs :
the dark enfolding road we leave behind

City of London

If we can hear the bells then we take their name,
if it's after The Hour then the bricks are closed,
if it's marked with the Arms we're locked in the centre
— *Lord, direct us* — along Queen Victoria Street,
Distaff Street, Old Fish Street Hill, where
the Walbrook trickles in florins & pence.

The men in luminous direct us upwards
— *Blackfriars Station, Major New Development* —
towards the City of Analogue. A thoroughfare of clocks
hedged with bronze eagles. The white pulse of Canary
Wharf flickers its amphetamine trip-switch but the City's
obelisk-mask has turned the day to stone.

At St Mary Woolnoth there's a Green Man in search
of global beers. THIS SYSTEM IS CONTROLLED
BY PERFECTUS. Staircases off King William Street
lead down past vectors to roofs beneath our feet
— *With a dead sound on the final stroke of nine* —
the river draws me to its future sources in the relics

of the lost — as if the holiday case has sprung & cast
its souvenirs along the A-road to the metropolitan camp.
A half-moon behind The Monument. A Vauxhall stops
and a man in uniform gets out at THE FINE LINE
restaurant. Turn left for DOCKLANDS. A courier
cuts a corner with an L-Plate on his tailpipe,

alert in a blacked-out visor. His sat nav is a clipboard
strung to handlebars & pegged to that : a folio A-Z
of London. His destination circled in HB. The walk
to Tower Bridge captures our shadow twelve times to hard
drive, two of which make laser-jet. Tourists complain
of commuters & talk of the limits of Health & Safety.

Pavements segue to staircase & pull us from the routes
we choose for ourselves, up ramps to roofs
with totem poles that ideogram the seven stages
of man, along a pedestrian runway of white offices
that display perfect desks of stationery but are, for this hour,
closed to us. A turnstile on black space that is locked.

White static runs to the reaches of ceramics & wires
as the river chants its out-takes. Someone has always
been here before : a stone-set foetal head, a clay offering,
is spooling sunlight on the wall of Oliver's warehouse.
Its flippers wind-up static, snout skewed,
eyeholes long bored into cavernous pistol shots.

Its body petrifies on a shingle of corks & clay pipes.
Its dumb weight — hollowed of intestine — trawls centuries
of river-beds. A crab leg pincers beneath a husk of brick —
when I lift that's all there is : a leg punked with fine barbs,
the motion of its amputation pistons towards the shoreline,
claws at the river, wipes without ligament in the breeze.

What the Courier Knows

3,011 interpreters along Whitehall

20,586 translators in The City

152 actuaries on the short stretch of Norton Folgate

12,701 code-makers for bank credits in Shoreditch

1,298,402 serotonin uplifters port-holed in blister-packs

312 languages in one metropolis, owners of numerical systems
& job descriptions

98,919 strip-owners of Visa in Chelsea

156,983 signature scrawls across unsecured cheques in Southwark

102,101 Blackberries like handheld cabs across Docklands

50,241 underarm toxins on Commercial Road

11,001 hotel swipe-cards in Bloomsbury

34,789 coiled ring-pulls on the Isle of Dogs

27,703 ex-east-enders in Dagenham

3,412 SIM cards plasticised inside Canary Wharf

742 new fragments of poetry on notebooks across 33 boroughs

8,041 units of ethanol consumed on Charing X Road

604 obsolete graffitoes on the Old Kent Road

30,312 minutes of conversation exchanged for billed tariff on Denmark Street (*I love you* spoken 989 times)

401 therapists in Golders Green

748,060,099 bones of the non-living weaving the Thames shoreline

312 languages, tongues like skinned dogs

ELEPHANT & CASTLE

It's a top-deck 176 situation at Elephant & Castle
the bottle rolls against my shoes
METHADONE 100ML. AILMENT 2 OF 14. MAY CAUSE
DROWSINESS. DO NOT OPERATE
MACHINERY OR DRINK ALCOHOL.
I can see everything from here except sobriety :
communities that have themselves bought-out in glass.

You only age like this in the all the time I don't see you :
so spend some time with us. Spend it like tokens
for kiosks that sell loose cigarettes. Spend it like drains.
Spend it like hard water down the Victorian water-mains.
Spend it like the Shard's doubling of stars. Spend it like
something light to read on the commuter's underpass :
A Beginner's Guide to Property & Culture.

Page 54 has a picture of an estate agent reading Chekhov
in a dressing room. If you don't see me tonight I got off
at the Nag's Head next to the Barclays.

And folded myself in the Night Safe for you.

MATT MERRITT

WARNING AGAINST USING THESE
POEMS AS A MAP

No scale is provided.
You are being left
to guess the exact distance

between what's said
and what was,
between a mere projection

onto the flat page
and a curved plane,
constantly in motion,

spinning through nothingness.
You are your own key.
Assign the appropriate value

to each symbol, and allow
the wide white spaces
to fill up with invisibles,

bloom with the language
of implication. Wait
for the words to accumulate

the sediment of meaning.

DESIRE LINES

*"Do not go where the path may lead, go instead where there is no path and leave a trail." – **Ralph Waldo Emerson***

Drought or drench draw them more clearly,
teach the secret geometry of hidden
or half-arsed purpose. For each

ribbon of rained-on intent,
tramped-down meander of resolve
that hardens into lane or jitty,

or even city street, another ten
remain as freehand scrawls, scribbles
at best, the chords and tangents

of long-forgotten arcs. A season's growth
softens edges, a work-crew and a one-off budget
tame the snake in the grass, or divide head

from tail, but a few days of scorching sun,
a week of winter, can reunite both
or sharpen the top-down perspective,

until each waste-ground's a history
of every passing idea and impulse, half-buried, half-
realised, but still being dreamed.

SVALBARD

Long, close August. We sleep with the window open to the street, wait for promised storms to cut the bullying heat back down to size. Cars clatter over sleeping policemen. Ambulances draw up at the nursing home, unhurriedly. Sometimes, we catch the cries of foxes in the cemetery, the ghost-written call and response of owls. And now wake to sounds, distant and rhythmic, I take for a flock of Canada Geese, migrating; a thing unheard of this side of the Atlantic. Only after several minutes does it become apparent, they're next door in our neighbour's bedroom. We lie, and wait for the ceiling rose to bloom, a sound widening between us in the cold ocean of the sheets, wondering if maybe it's the man we've seen painting her front door and carrying flat-packs in from the car, listening as a tailwind takes them faster and higher, out over the flow country, Cape Wrath, the firths, calling to maintain contact across the wide North Sea, descending now to Svalbard, the mountains bright with meltwater, the tundra with saxifrage, crowberry, bell-heather, in the 3a.m. sunlight of the Arctic summer.

WATCHING WOODCOCKS, 25.4.10

The birdwatcher's problem becomes the poet's.

How to remain within the frame, yet unobserved,
how to frame something that is in a moment
more bat than bird,
more branch than bat,
more leaf-mould than branch.

How to sift countless stories;
a bird *witlesse* enough to be trodden on
yet capable of carrying its young
away from danger on its back, a bird
that escapes the dog days
by flying to the moon.

How to use that prized pin-feather;
for fishing-flies, for fans, for removing
motes from eyes. In ancient China,
for stimulating the clitoris.
For painting woodcocks
flickering at the edge of vision.

How to make yourself
more camera than birdwatcher or poet
before you are gone
into the black bead of its eye.

THE ELEPHANT IN THE ROOM

is an elephant. Far from ignoring it,
we are trying to recall exactly how it snuck in here,
how long we have before it strips the house-plants,

hose-pipes its trunk to one of the bath-taps
to satisfy its extraordinary demands, or turns the furniture
    to kindling
with us still on it. Of course! This whole ramshackle edifice

must have been built around its great grey bulk.
Did I say grey? It tends towards
a textbook shade, but occasionally colours

pink or white, depending on the progress of the evening,
the quality of the light. Every knock on the door these days
seems to be a dung beetle, but even they

are beginning to doubt their ability to keep pace
with production. The creature turns one huge, deaf ear
to their mutterings, tunes the other in to every conversation

and later joins the ongoing debate as a vigorous advocate
of its own highly-structured and stable social order.
It is unafraid to trumpet its species' many virtues

but has been known to settle for the *sotto voce* denigration
of hippopotami and all their works. In this current state,
a periodic outbreak of vicious, indiscriminate

but rationalised rage known as *musth*, it fears nothing
– not mouse, nor man, nor umbrella stand. To banish it
to the far savannah of your conscious mind and pray

for the thunder of ivory-smugglers' guns might feel like the only
viable strategy, but it has already weighed your worth
and found you wanting. Don't expect it will ever forget.

YELLOWHAMMERS

Snow brings them in off the fields. That's all.
Impatient for the lifting of its veil,
see two, gaudy as canaries in the rowan

with winter's first fall untrodden on the lawn.
Not since, maybe, four Christmases ago,
when one flew full tilt into the kitchen window

but in minutes picked itself up and was gone
before the sleeping cats could catch on,
have they... but no. No, that's a lie.

Not since the day you died,
in fact, and that sudden buoyant swarm
appeared from nowhere to warm

next door's leylandii. No pretence
or grand goodbyes, and even then no change of tense
as we talked on and on, while they – little tongues of fire –

flickered against the dank green spires,
impatient for the lifting of the veil.
Snow brings them in off the fields. That's all.

DAVID MORLEY

from FRESH WATER

in memory of Nicholas Ferrar Hughes, 1962–2009

PORT MEADOW, OXFORD, 1983

Walking to Woodstock Road from Wytham Wood
where leaf-worlds welled from all the wood's wands,
we talked salmon, midges, floodmeadows, the energy system
cindering softly under us, slow-cooking the marshlands.
The gate ought to be here. The map said so.
That map back at my flat... Look, there's a spot
somewhere this way where sheep shove through.
See those fieldfares and redwings? They landed last night.
Then a step within a fence nobody bothered with for years
or knew, except the sheep. So Nick stepped up
and through, and there on the other side, two horses
with thrilled-up ears, barged him skilfully to a stop.
I said that gate was around here – pointing a mile or two.
Worth the way – Nick's arms across both horses – *to know these two.*

DRAGONFLIES

This water's steep and deep. There are signs in artery red.
Their letters pump with advice. But it's June and we have trod
ourselves senseless sampling some imaginary species of
    coleoptera…

So, there are our cautions slung down like life-vests by the river
and with stone-drop certainty we launch out from a hanging ledge
to collide with a chill so stinging it was like flinging your body
into a bank of nettles. Then head-butting the surface to see
at eyelash-level the whiphands of Common Backswimmers
surge and sprint, each footing a tiny dazzle to prism.
                              Then these
sparking ornaments hovering then islanding on our shoulders
each arching its thorax into a question: what is the blue
that midnights all blue? How can crimson redden before you?
The old map mutters that Here Be Dragons, and it lies.

Here be Darters, Skimmers, drawn flame. Here, are Dragonflies.

THE WATER MEASURER

We could have watched him until our watches rusted on our wrists
or the tarn froze for the year's midnight. The Water Measurer
struck his pose and recalibrated his estimates as if he had misplaced
his notebook, or perhaps his mind, with all that staring at water.

Why does he walk on it with such doubt and mismeasure
when he has the leisure of hydrophobia (those water-fearing hairs
on the undersides of his legs)? Maybe that is his secret,
that he doesn't know his step will never or not quite penetrate
the depth below, glowing with prey and the upturned eyes
of predators. Does he ever get any of this right? Is he unwise?

He tests and counts, counts and tests, in pinprick manoeuvres,
never satisfied with the data of darkness or statistics of sunlight.
It seems he holds his nose at the thought of getting it right, or of not
getting it not right, never or not quite like the water-fly in *Hamlet*.

from A LIT CIRCLE

DEMELZA DO-IT-ALL

After my act as barrel-walker there's my turn on the silver
    thread, more subtle
than my work with fantailed doves or the performing dogs
    or hoop-tossing.
I do ten acts solo, six more with my sister starring as *The
    Starlight Sisters*.

I look in that mirror with that big hundred-watter and I don't
    know myself.

That's eleven different names, that's sixteen costume changes
    and they say
we don't work hard. That's what the police said when they
    gave the Court Order.
'Left the matter in our hands'. One day's notice to strike camp
    and shove off.

The act with the glitterball, that's my favourite, when I'm up
    in that steel star
swirling sixty spins a minute for a full two minutes, and that
    glitterball's
spattering silver stars over my body until I'm almost imaginary.
    Dazzling.

What's hardest is a hurt, sprains say, crying cramped in the
    caravan for weeks
overhearing applause from the canvas through the open door,
    that's pain,
or hearing the claps of rain on the van's roof when the show's
    over.

I was down in the industrial estate with my sister for small
    animal food,
the vet for the dogs. There are swastikas scratched on every
    circus poster.

COLIN CLOWN

On every circus poster, let's face it, my face. Not Mick's face.
    Not Mike's face.
Why is that? Is it because I am so handsome? You can say
    that again. Is it
because I am so handsome? There's international clown code
    in that decision.
Each clown has his face painted on to an eggshell and no two
    eggs are alike.
Which is why I'm up in lights on the town's lampposts and
    not Mick or Mike.

I've heard some horror stories about this town. Have you
    heard the one
about the bent coppers? In the end they used pliers. I've been
    promoted.
Mick and Mike got nabbed with their mitts in the mopus, so.
    I am Pierrot.

Arlecchino, Pierrot and Auguste. Mike and Mick swiped the
    first parts
but I was an august Auguste. I was the straight man the
    audience likes
who catches the first pie or bucket but doesn't pine or make
    a racket.

I am Arlecchino. Where is Auguste now? I am afraid of Mick
    and Mike
but their faces lied. They work somewhere dead now, like
    Shropshire.

What's that noise? Is the cat at the door or the wind? Or
the wind's cats?
My face is clean. My hands are clean. I'm dead. It's
raining dogs out there.

MOOLÒ THE MUSICIAN

Where's Moolò? Here's Moolò. Why are you calling when I
am here
where I always go, stage-left of ringside with my tin cymbal,
snare drum,

tin whistle, my sweet loops of music, my white lies of
sound that make
the big top vibrate or slow to silence when the silver thread's
being strode?

Under my thumb the beat of the red drum and the
applause ripening.

Woodpigeons unhinge from the hedgerows. Where the beasts
were bedded
there are scraps spilled from the floors of heaven. Magpies
spy and spring.

Curlews collect long keys to their low homes between the
burnt grass.
Lapwings manage their manic marriages, low-diving,
upside-downing.

One trodden ring. Yellow grass. Green grass. Black grass.
Where's Moolò?

I am here where I always go, stage-left
of ringside with my tin cymbal,
snare drum, tin whistle.
Under my thumb
the beat of the
red drum

and the applause of wide England where beasts come first
and last.

Here you are standing centre.   Here, in this circle of grass.
Caught song, caught sound, caught art, caught light, caught air.

ALISTAIR NOON

from EARTH RECORDS

10

Late at night the Balkan languages clog
at Horgos, where they wait to gain admittance
to the circle of stars. A see-through smog
surrounds the returners from the remittance
economy: static, running exhausts
and the world's greatest mass cigarette break,
as coaches queue up for one of the ports,
bays with a quay, where the night shift's awake.
We hoot, or cheer each inch; the wise just doze.
No border guard knows the meaning of *soon*.
Priština, Niš to Dortmund, Ulm. One goes
to Mariampol. (*O beautiful moon
of Mariampol*… Sat in East Berlin,
Bobrowski looked up.) Here's Europe. We're in.

34

An endless machine moulds the acetate
we listen to, scoring earth as it blasts
the uncooperative hills to create
and kill while it rolls the ground flat, and casts
a dark, flowing carpet of pungent tar,
pressing black grooves that don't turn about
one point but run straight on, each single car
a new stylus whose sound fades in, then out,
as you stand on this stony riverbed,
risking the seasonal rush and flood
of mountain rains avalanching ahead,
laying out their extra tarmac of mud,
roaring you along this temporary drain
to concerts of streets on the soundless plain.

ALL THOSE OLD APARTMENT BLOCKS

All those old apartment blocks
from Magdeburg to Vladivostok
still herd mostly with their kind.
They wait in one long sullen line,
in sun and snow, hail and rain,
for a firework show of paint.

All know how their walls once were.
Now they leave for where they've heard
new lifts, lights and loos are stocked,
and ask, with one eye fixed on the clock,
the next in the new line, queuing still,
to keep their place until they've reskilled.

Soft blue, pale green, beige and cream
absorb, as grey before, all sunbeams.
Onto those walls the rain still drops,
snow dissolves, every hailstone breaks.
The starter question: *Which will you take?*
Walls for life, or paint in the shops?

PABLO NERUDA IN AYLESBURY

I walk through you now as if crossing
a rope bridge into the mist,
a hare creeping back to a habitat,
keeping to the bushes as a red kite
glides overhead. You're a pitch-black room
I used to live in, a surface familiar
and strange to the touch.

Fragmenting clouds patrol the estates.
The grandchildren of Camden, Barbados, the Punjab,
Calabria, Cochin, Glasgow and Newcastle
chat in the terraces and the semi-detached dream.
Rains commute back every few hours,
a break between gardening programmes.
This week we're in the Home Counties.

As far as we'll get from any cliffs or beach,
end of a Grand Union tentacle
and an iron road to the imperial capital.
Fruit I had no need to peel,
streets I learnt like a mother-tongue,
I knew you before I could read maps.

Your roads trace Dark Age furlongs,
roundabouts — a cyclical view of history.
When I dig down into your earth I find
a ritually smashed-in skull.
When I stagger from your pubs at midnight I meet
a ritual of smashed-in faces.
I hear the bad punk song of your name in the White Swan.
Synthpop seeps into my ears. Howard Jones, are you there?
Bright records in a windswept backstreet
condensed into CDs in the warm centre.

I cycle the Amber Way towards
the Buckinghamshire Samurai.
We see through each other outside Smiths.
I have my tokens and tickets.

THE SEAFARER POET IN NEWCASTLE

I had ridden a cloud-horse to that kingdom,
but the gate-guards wouldn't let me ride home.
So voyage-worn were the edges of my mirror-book
that the reflection might not've been my own.

A Friday in early March, around sundown,
and the local women were out in their bikinis.
All I had till the wheel-beast rumbled off to London
was a Guinness and a song-bag of Seamus Heaney's.

So I boarded the rail-whale to Jarrow
and strolled to the sea's fingertips where I found
enough flotsam to hammer up a water-arrow
that would've humbled any Anglian mound.

It was my quick Kon-Tiki to re-state
a theory whose truth I already knew.
Back the route some of us came, I sailed
on a brine-flight no longer quite new.

It was cold in that life-image in March,
and my stomach read each trough and crest.
It was damp in that wave-steed and I started
to feel its hooves moving below my chest.

For Chris Jones

MATT NUNN

OF SEX AND GARDENS

In sex and blossoming green,
we catch the most we can
of the ringing light as it spells
'Forever' out upon the golden fathoms
of romantic youth,
and yes, goddammit, even poetry,
and having nothing to say no to.

Before the grief of September distance
and the inevitable arriving of rearranging rain
smelting a stinging sadness
onto an unknown bleary sun
that'll cover us in blubbing,
we should rewrite our magic faces
in its bulbs of borrowed eternity.

To Louisa Ryland

Blessed to be born as one of
your zillion grot-face nippers
splattered in ashes of the Cole
who have grazed in an obscure corner
of your Municipal Republic of green sprawling dreams,

I thank thee for giving us voluminous blooms flourishing,

leaving us the lungs in which to breathe in pure.

For planting us a tight spot
in a land of dense industrial mass
to grow the blessed-out lyricism
of two centuries of space.

*Louisa Ann Ryland (1814 - 1889) was a major benefactor who donated
large areas of land that were used to create public parks in Birmingham.
The largest of these, donated in 1873, was some 80 acres and became
Cannon Hill Park.*

M50 Poem

Driving with the murderous eyes of Tudor-haired truckers
between fields of forever gentle zoos missing some familiar notes
but ragrolled with ghosts washed up from an estuary
whilst being kissed by the chill of the sunshine
winking off the potholes with flat lemonade sparkle,
there cannot be a Paranoid Android on here
slaloming the broken queues of traffic
who, in the midst of speeding with existential confusion,
has never felt the sensation of time being harshly erased
then feeling it reappearing further along
this road composed in rainbow and bruises,
scattered and in the wrong order.

LONG MYND, NEW YEAR'S DAY

No, there ain't no god to fix us,

so we drift, chewed up and flobbed out
from between the jaw-line of battering weather
and flaming expletives swirling abusively
down from the angry Black Mountains,
pausing only to pull moonies into the void
and for you to sprinkle erratically,

until we trip over ourselves, kiss
the high sky of sheep and fall
onto our muck-splattered throne
to feel our bonces, gone rotten with booze,
blast off over the valley

and watch cloud moods clear smoothly, daubing
oozes of sun onto people awakening
to the fabulous shades of hope gathering.

This could be a fucking brilliant year.

MARIO PETRUCCI

halves

the blade drops
& both half-oranges
rock upon their backs as

beetled species made
zestful but without
the frantic legs

enlarged in heat
to overbrightly dribble
sap in that broken moment

after insect sex which could be
love yet dictates each rolls
apart to undercarriage

straight-grained ex
-posed in falling apart
where one gains access

to tarter matters animal
or vegetable softly to
be consumed for

rind is hard on us
unscooped or what
the starveling leaves

behind or am I for
getting I was once in
heart fruit-perfect & un-

halved?

for Pablo Neruda

today my life you

fell through me – light no longer subject
to longing or dismay as if dusks & dawns
had melled then recombined – one object
sight purifies in just that way a bloom

in darkness is no less for never being seen
as I am held in deeper swoons daytimes blur
knowing flowed-through nows come clear
in fragrance nocturnes prise – even mine –

too late to dam the river your perfume swings
vastly & by night over my steep levee   or stem
those aromatics your upward-flowing lingering
fingers climb Muscat-wise through brain –

through bright sleep I groaned for others to make
awakening – in time your waters flood my water slaking
blood depthless in fervent – till we embrace & glory be
you lower yourself relentlessly light gently upon me

See: Cien sonetos de amor (XLIX)

anima I

cannot write
her straight – this
man in whom straightness is

an arrow curving
its path : mere illusion
for lovers who plot where it arcs

I cannot know
her in this line I draw
back tauter than the string that lets

pain go or
the bow supple in its
bend yet ever prone to warp & send

off-true : so
how may I find a You
where speech is impossible unless

this skimming
of targets be the way
into speaking between a man &

that woman he
started with neither
mother nor wife but She he

squints at
clear through near
-sighted morning as if
her stroke

steady & precise
through him were

all
air ready
to be parted

nearness of lovers

tight on the Tube
so
close the soft thrust

of the train bitters my
lip
on the twill of his right

shoulder
i smell the second waft
of her

breathed
aroma white with tended
teeth

reserved
for him received by this
stranger

who suddenly loves
before
her beau can

that wateriness
in blue
as her still

eyes
unblock something

of me
through him
&
i hear in thunder

wheels upon wheels
his
small gasp to the rock

of her carriage : words
intended
for one nuzzled other

urgency spills as
love
does – as love

does

small love poem

& all the big things
half-said

their immense machineries
seized

the state with its tense angels
pleased

till none sings except in dread
i ask

instead what love cannot say
yet

gleans as heart's squat flask
yields

illimitless in & out in
fist

-sized gulps of
world

seas

JEREMY REED

FLEET

A black network in London's thalamus,
a landscaped-over solid trawl
licking a trace into Dead Dog Basin,
like a path-lab procedure,
a subterranean autopsy

of body parts in soup, bottles and dogs,
a swirly ooze down to Kentish Town loch
and under to St Pancras,
furred arteries pushing to King's Cross
as cold bacterial soup, a mucky rush

that puddles on the road sometimes
in thunder-rain at Holborn and Blackfriars
in think-bubbles, the river's secret life
come up to be decoded like intelligence
and splashed through by the tube exit,

I'll never know I've walked it home
in squidgy traces on the floor
at South Hill Park like a liquid barcode.
We talk about the river's drop
at the Magdala, drunk out of the rain

in leaf-slidy November, the street
wallpapered over by stripped orange leaves;
and someone claims they've fucked beside its source,
the bottomless pool by the aqueduct
power-pointing into the river

to feel its drive into the underground,
but it's not clear where water starts,
unlike a road, its shoplifting impulse
traffics into a dark gritty corridor.
We stand above it as we talk,

a disturbed system of tunnels and tubes,
aquifers, islanded from the rain,
and I can feel the drop under my feet
into the Fleet pit, as I buy a round
and feel the fourth or fifth light up my brain.

WENLOCK ARMS

A summer there in sticky warehouse heat,
our fuzzy light-polluted sweat-drenched thrust
to monetize a dead friend's books
boxed into dusty architectural blocks,
dealers categorising firsts and states
Red Snapper partners itchy for hot cash
both of us maintaining dandified looks
in repurposed high-end Shoreditch,
its rogue outtake the Wenlock Arms
looking like a Krays' gang operation,
peeling green walls, purple frontage —
I'd knock at 10am for Aaron's flaky need
to stabilize, a drinks top-up
kicking the pineal with a sugared boot.
12 handpumps, a stripped-down defiant room
yeasty with real ale, I stepped into
a throwback parallel space-time
scrutinized for my beret and paste rings
crowding in starburst clusters at the bar —
an edgy glitter, a moody lagoon.
She never spoke, just handed me the glass.
Two months, two hours a day deconstructing
solid book tons as physicals, we sold
into profit — I kept a CA shelf
of Robert Duncan, orange sunshine
stored in the pages, had a last drink there
like flipping back to 1958.

Got all my times wrong, bussed back into town.
Knowing I'd be too early, or too late.

Norton Folgate

Dick stick-up Turpin's parish, bandit dude,
no plastic, only bling and flash,
a leather wristlock grabbing cash,
a gun snouting the carotid's
blipping quasar, he'd strip them nude

if they resisted force. On Folgate Street
the light arriving seems to stay
like time-cutting video:
are the photons full of spatial info
the same dusty ones I saw yesterday

as gold-polluted dazzle, carbon haze?
Dick sniffs for J.P. Morgan, stiffs
investment bankers, wears a black eye-patch
and rips them like a virtual alligator
or a Tornado GR4

nuking a shelled Libyan tank.
Dick's the beef in Bishopsgate,
his fat cat's cock turns gold in Blossom Street
slashing metabolised profits at a wall
hallucinating 1739

rope-burn cutting into his twisted neck
hoisted to the mobster Tyburn gallows,
the crowd big as an O2 revival gig,
his loot stashed away like WMD,
the thing like a psychotic episode

only it's happening. He lopes
into the Water Poet for troubleshooters,
the black pavement grid outside rumbling streams
as the city's diagnostic read-out
of its bacterial anthology.

His dealing room's his killing field;
spread-betting while thunder slams in
as fizzy atmospheric dialect,
a black slash over Spital Square,
breaking that moment into violent rain.

WHITEHALL ENDGAME

(depleted uranium mix)

The 5pm sky's like rainy sapphires
a blue toxic hydrocarbon blanket,
and you're my pick-up, bite my lip
to redden like a strawberry.
It's later in accelerated endgame time
by 600 seconds than when we met
at the compressed Starbucks on Hollen Street,
you a Beijing space-time interloper
put into a blonde-bobbed Eurasian mix.

The psychopathic jackal Tony Blair,
four blacked-out Range Rovers gunned
through town, a war criminal's carbon tail
choking polluted haze, his handgun grin
cold as forensics, czar to every war's
genocide, the killer autocrat
smeared in depleted uranium, Gulf blood,
the meltdown hedge funder — the commandant
guarded 24/7 by thugs in suits,
Glock pistols in their Paul Smith repertoire.

We watch his cars open a corridor
into a cannibalistic future —
Blair crunches Cherie for a final meal.
The day builds on us like a pyramid
of neural info — *love me to the end
of Soho village* — there's no other way
sighting those tyres that leave blood on the bend.

DANIEL SLUMAN

ABANDON

Your body is snapping back into shape,

stomach as smooth as an envelope
as I sleep in my cot, a tiny bomb

fattening with your future. You stretch

your teenage bones over the hospital sheets,
surrounded by the mute applause of Hallmark.

This alimony of feeling won't shake,

you make a choice; there is a sparrow
outside the window, it twitches its head

upwards & whips into the empty sky.

LOVE SONG TO A TUMOUR

When they ripped you from me
I saw a greasy bundle of fireworks,

nature's atom bomb. It's not the impact
which hurts, but the fall-out that settles

like fibreglass in my eyes; I see the entropy
in everything, the date printed in my blood,

a loose thread stitched in the lining of my lungs.
At night we pull the bone-cluttered duvet over us,

our shadows slide like clothes thrown on a lampshade.

EVOCATION

Her name is a fat fuse
tensed between your teeth,

greased with possibilities

that rise & fall like the pale arc
of her hips. You swallow & she is smoke

easing through your muscles

as you soothe the car to the lights.
At green, the clutch chokes & you sling

past the crossroads like a weight

has evaporated; as if something
was leaning on the brakes

all this time.

Dear Samaritans, I'm writing this to let you know that everything's okay now

The last time we spoke

I was smearing the red flag
of myself around the tub;

the bottle & knife clinking

in my hand. I mentioned
that since I was a child

I have been narrowing

all the questions in the world
to matchsticks, striking them

against my skull, I don't know
how I felt nothing so utterly.

I've learnt patience,
not everything has to wisp

from my fingers. There is a priest
who prays for me; they fly

off his knuckles & hang in the air,

swooping, their feathers
line my pillow. If he could see

these gaping white smiles

on my arm, could taste
the dreams that split my sleep,

he'd understand. God sees me

as a tiny pink coffin, wandering

from place to place, waiting
to fall into the open earth.

DEDICATION

'the more I live the more I think
two people together is a miracle'
        — Adrienne Rich

Jeff Buckley's soul steams
from the speakers downstairs,

where you hum, shuffling in your slops,

dropping bacon in hot oil, dashing cutlery
on an epiphany of china.

*

My mind settles like a spun coin

warbling to silence. The fresh intimacy
of your sheets is a currency

I'll fritter on cheap flimsy words;

if you cleaved me in two
you'd smell your perfume on my bones.

MARIA TAYLOR

SHE IS HERE

The train's ragged movement suits
her bones, the view is mother's ruin,
a concrete map of haphazard streets;
White City, Westway, Wormwood.

No one saw her pass with a bag
through the ticket barriers, no one
saw her ride the bloodline through
the city. She is seventeen, invisible.

The words she was taught to speak
are strung from asphalt and pitch,
now she'll meet the world head-on,
it will speak a different language.

LARKIN

I

September. Someone hands me a copy of Larkin,
thirty eager teenage faces search me for clues.
I will love teaching Larkin, I will embrace Larkin,
'A' Level Syllabi, York Notes, Spark Notes;
we're going to crack this Larkin like a walnut.

II

October. Larkin has moved in. My photographs
are all of Larkin, the face on the television
belongs to Larkin. In the crisp mornings
birds are tweeting *Larkin! Larkin! Larkin!*
It's Sunday lunchtime, thirty essays on Larkin
scream at me. *Was Larkin a misogynist?*
Was Larkin a misanthrope? Was Larkin a joker?
I give up and go in search of food. Larkin passes me
the leeks and compliments me on my choice of wine.

III

The term ends. We have done our Christmas quiz
on Larkin. 'I hate Larkin,' says a small girl with eczema.

IV

'Tis the season to be Larkin. I go home with a suitcase
full of Larkin. On Boxing Day I drink brandy
and salute Larkin. I think I'm going Larkin.

V

Last night when I was asleep, Larkin was on top
of me again, grunting. His lenses were all steamed-up,
he enjoys the feel of the living, the way we move.
I fended him off with a hardback of *New Women Poets*
and woke up, relieved to see someone else.

VI

You may turn over and begin. Mr. Larkin is your invigilator
for today. I raise my hand, 'How do you spell MCMXIV?'
He clips the back of my ear with a shatterproof ruler.
I draw a Smurf in the margin, I have forgotten everything
there is to know about Larkin. He gives up on me and leaves.
Larkin's shoes echo noisily through the gym.

VII

August. Twisted. They're opening little envelopes,
some smile, some cry. A photographer from the local paper
takes photos of students throwing Larkin in the air.
I'm better now, cured of Larkin. The girl with eczema
has a lighter. I find a charred copy of *High Windows*
behind the gym with a used condom and a can of Lilt.
Never such innocence, as I think someone once said.

MR. HILL

For Patricia

For a while he's gone back to his first wife,
who's decided to keep him on a mantelpiece
with mouth-blown vases on either side.
It means she's had to speak to his mistress.
They have more in common than she realised,
but wonders if her toenails are still painted red.
No one is quite sure where to scatter him,
not her, not their ne'er-do-well grown-up kids,
not even the lady with scarlet toenails.

His wife sits in a sea-fret of white mist,
sighing through her thick cigarette smoke,
she is so confused, she even asks me,
but I'm only a neighbour. For years I thought
he'd already died, the way she spoke of him.
Mrs. Hill takes another drag, decides to post
him back to his lady friend, confiding in me
even though he's dead, he's still a bastard.

THE SUMMER OF CONTROLLED EXPERIMENTS

From their awkward position on the field
the skies overhead spell tedium,
an anxious flapping of wings breaks out,
a form of inverse applause.

One of the experimenters vows never again
to wear a dress shaped like a downturned tulip
so unflattering and bulbous at the hip,
without the cover of a cardigan.

Both have noted the dip in temperature
and are discussing supper, no candle lights,
this gnawing need for something bigger.

They walk home in the frowsy rays of dusk,
a palm pressed against a palm
but this is no holy kiss,
they are leading each other to the exit.

In Love

First, dream yourself into a mid-terrace
let flowers grow inside your head.

Rethink the kitchen, see a dining table
tangled with jasmine, petals over tired pine.

Where once you were arm-deep in sink grease,
watch holy roses grow from a plughole

as swallowtails escape from a cutlery drawer
and fly up to a room, not quite your own.

Here are laelia, risen from an unwashed duvet
a mirror all dew, names written in breath.

SIMON TURNER

QUIVERS

for Rochelle

That robin's so bolshy, plucking suet pellets
clean out of our hands like it's the easiest,
the most natural thing. Cautious enough, yes,
when the wind's gotten up, and the jasmine
by the back door flails its lunatic tendrils.
But on a clear day in March, when the sun's out,
and the forsythia's bright as a photoflash,
there's no stopping him. Yet he's so delicate
when he comes in to feed – just a quick fuss of air
from his wings, his feet sensed for barely an instant
as pinpricks on the skin of my upturned palm
before he spins in mid-air and zips back to the trees.
And what about the daffodils, coming into bloom
without warning, both of us listening to music
in the room upstairs, those drab green buds erupting
in a dazzle of yellow on the cluttered dining table?
There must be a name for these everyday miracles.
If not, I'll spend tomorrow morning thinking one up,
and write you a note to let you know my findings.

At Kenilworth

Tell me,
what did you find
at the top of the hill,
on the rutted trail
towards Chase Lane?

Only the big sky,
& a clutch of trees thriving
behind the tumbled wall,
where the gelding press
rusts amongst rubble.

Tell me,
how did it look,
the castle, from that height,
at that distance,
through the mizzling rain?

Blasted & hollow,
its walls the dulled copper
of the moon in eclipse
on a cloudless evening
amid a fury of stars.

& tell me,
how did it feel
to have the wind shake you,
to scream right through you
& clatter your bones?

It was like rare music
pouring in through the heart
& jigging the soul from its ease,
or flocked birds gushing
into an empty tree to roost.

PLAINSONG

i.m. Frank Robinson

This city has changed so much in less than a decade
& when I was still living here the changes were constant:
tramlines etched in the road, the public square remodelled,
new bars, new stores, new luxury flats which most people
who lived in Nottingham would never have been able to afford.

So many changes that whenever I come back here as a visitor
after living elsewhere for a year or two, I have the sensation
of being a very old man, my memories of the city so outdated
that they seem to me like newsreel footage from a different era –
grainy monochrome, cut-glass BBC announcers, the works.

But I'll admit that some of the changes have been for the better,
& I feel no real sense of loss except the loss I feel for Frank,
the Xylophone Man who played for the crowds in the city centre,
the wordless plainsong of his voice wavering like a mass of sparrows
above the fractured glassy notes he struck upon his instrument.

He sang & played purely for the joy of it, plus a little spare change,
& had nothing to play & nothing to sing except the joy of living.
There's a plaque dedicated to him at the spot where he busked,
& the people I've spoken to remember him extremely fondly:
his absence is felt throughout the city like the loss of a vital faculty.

DIGITAL BIRMINGHAM

a Google poem for George Ttoouli

Birmingham is Britain's second largest city
Birmingham is the birthplace of Cadbury's chocolate
Birmingham is the home of the balti
Birmingham is a shopper's paradise
Birmingham is twinned with Frankfurt
Birmingham is made up of three elements
Birmingham is split into seven quarters
Birmingham is derived from *Beorma ingas Ham*
Birmingham is on a roll
Birmingham is over the moon
Birmingham is full of surprises
Birmingham is interdisciplinary
Birmingham is renowned for it
Birmingham is very much a work in progress
Birmingham is a snowy city
Birmingham is a luxurious city
Birmingham is a burgeoning city
Birmingham is a rock music city
Birmingham is a fantastic city
Birmingham is a global city
Birmingham is a Fairtrade city
Birmingham is a bustling city
Birmingham is a young city
Birmingham is a green city
Birmingham is a spectacular city
Birmingham is a difficult city
Birmingham is subject to regular external scrutiny
Birmingham is often overlooked

Birmingham is very much open to debate
Birmingham is expanding
Birmingham is delighted
Birmingham is driven
Birmingham is working
Birmingham is here
Birmingham is often
Birmingham is quite
Birmingham is blue
Birmingham is missing
Birmingham is not the only one
Birmingham is as peachy as this woman's jumper
Birmingham is a family run business
Birmingham is the greatest place in the world

TRACY'S FACE

The city
is more beautiful
than it has a right
to be –

some mornings, even
a chucked white mattress
propped on garbage & huddled weeds
is luminous

more beautiful than
Rita Hayworth
easing off black
silk gloves in *Gilda*

beeches with sticky
newborn leaves
are charged with green
electricity

or Grace Kelly packing
or unpacking hers or
Jimmy Stewart's suitcase
in *Rear Window*

concrete cylinders
of uncertain purpose
contend with the sky
& achieve themselves

or Julianne Moore
anxious on the clinic steps
before broad glass doors
brimful of autumn blood

a tree goes crazy
with silver laser-light:
tramlines slink
downhill in the dark

or Gershwin rolling easy
through Manhattan's alleys
like blown Atlantic snow
or yesterday's *New York Times* –

& generous: so much light,
& objects massed
around a mobile core;
the choppy, ravenous eye

My Rejection Slips (4)

Dear Simon,

I am writing to inform you of a change in my material circumstances: the printed page, alas, is no longer commensurate to my needs, & I have therefore been forced to expand my operations beyond its confines. These days I am far more likely to take the form of the moon in daylight, smudged on the blue like the ghost of a fingerprint; or the music made by hammered metal & breaking glass in a wrecker's yard beside the canal, than that of the ode or the sonnet or the villanelle. Please understand that this is nothing personal, simply a recognition of the inherent limitations of the language we've been given, & I would be glad to give you the number of a colleague of mine who comes highly recommended, & who specialises in melancholy epiphanies at sunset. I wish you every success in all you do.

Yours sincerely,

The Poem

DEBORAH TYLER-BENNETT

LEAPING BARONET

*In which Squire Mytton vaults a dining table on Baronet,
his one-eyed horse ...*

Mytton spans history's dining table, cartoon
mount all spindled legs, matched only
by cock-eyed surprise.
Tinkling barley-twist stemmed glasses,
etched decanters
                reflect hooves, silver puddled,
trays joggled to lunacy's straining beat.

Beloved in pub prints, feat
to draw punters, wooden
Squire bests dining-table's length
on rocking-mare made flesh.

Some penny-plains half-capturing
lips' curve, rapturous,
eyes distended with wild joy.

Deep lines etch peg-doll face, betraying
how he'd live, re-live that jump again,
Bedlam's Tam O'Shanter, no hag
pursuing, through heart's fast-buckling terrain.

*Note: Squire John 'Mango' ('Mad Jack') Mytton (1796–1834), was one
of the most popular Regency figures to be depicted in sporting prints,
books, and paintings. A hard-drinking eccentric who rushed across duck
ponds naked in order to get a better shot at birds, rode a pet bear through
his dining room, he was also known for his many accidents (setting
himself alight to cure hiccups) as well as his sporting prowess. He died of
drink, after spending his last years as a debtor.*

Rude Boy

You couldn't make him up ...

If occupying photography's age
he'd be smeared blur, man
of several heads and hands,
seat occupied by human smudgery,
spirit image exiting a scullery.

Carry On's Sir Rodney Ffing (with two 'f's),
Sir Sid Ruff Diamond, breasting disorder
on a bear, saluting thinnest air,
ignoring quaked company, ball-and-claw chairs
scant shielding guests. Let's

face it, any séance waking him'd
feature more than double knocking,
carpets worn by heels a-drumming,
yells, view halloos, low bellows,
sudden raucous laughter mocking
till redundant, shy:
                    'Is anybody there?'

Smeary, blurred, lost room's sigh.

FLOYD ON EXITING

I.M.: Keith Floyd, 1943–2009 / William Gibson, 1884–1955

When Keith Floyd died,
tabloid story: CHEF'S FINAL FEAST
(partridge, cocktails, full-blown wine)
reminded Mum of Billy Gibson's partied going
(bitter, dessert cake, marinated song)
at Sutton Lib Club's *Pensioners' Christmas Night*.

Billy poling up come dawn's glazed light, trilby tight-
balanced at crown's back, wrong
scarf ... Piquantly 'worse for wear',
boasting booze too much, food too much,
'fantastic times' tasted. Such
swanning served later by friends, their
glacé eyes. He'd sung: *Let him go, let him tarry,*
let him sink, let him swim'.
'Suffer tomorrow', Daughter grinned
at forced defiance. 'Your head'll be
that old chestnut: THE DRUNKARD'S CURSE'.

Mates re-heated Billy's refused
seat downstairs, he'd felt abused,
well-meaning Steward, ill-versed
in tact, asked: 'Able-bodied?' Boozing
upstairs, dying-up to 'Showman' nick-name,
ballad's flambéd flame.
Gone in bed, no bruising
hang-over, cure un-needed.

Now, Floyd's obituary note,
mean-spirited rival gloats
of days mis-lived. Still, something to be said
for tables left post- savoured food and drink,
hung-over insecurities dwindled (think
reducing stock). Obits gut and joint the dead,
no cognac after-glow …

Fabled feasts feed hungry ghosts, allow
my unrepentant Angel's chorus: *'Let him tarry, let him go.'*

BROWN TOWN ELEGY

For Lucy and Elsie Bean

Things change, as you look.

Leaning Butcher's outhouse,
sweet-shop's ribcage sighing
on toppling brick chest, head lowering.
Tin ads (*Dairymaid*) spore gathering,
sentinel cachou bottles on counters
no one's owning anymore.

Set off now, what's left to gawp at?
Car parks where *Croft Infants* glowered.
Raising the sneck, don't recognise
Great Granddad Billy's garden, *grande-guignol*
gnomes gone, stable where he toiled
as the people's vet bricked up.

When I was a kid we lived there,
smelling his tobacco come Sundays,
polishing medals won by long-buried dogs.
Playgrounds echo familiar names:
'Crofties', 'Weeds', 'Lawns', 'Lammas'
now 'Brown Town', 'Smack City',
needles dotting summer grass.

I know them gone, but Saturdays have me fooled.

Outside a villa where saloon cars park,
Great Aunt Lucy's on bended knee,
red-leading mosaic stoops.

Raises turbaned head considering
who might come up the drive,
if to let them, not wanting muddy
complications. Leave her kneeling.

Things change,
Billy's garden smart with chimes,
sun-loungers, plastic squirrels,
gothic gnomes removed. Gone, Lucy,
ninety-five summers' tenant.

Still I see her, bending at the step,
unappreciative of visitors who'll muck it,
tiny figure wobbling in the sun.

TONY WILLIAMS

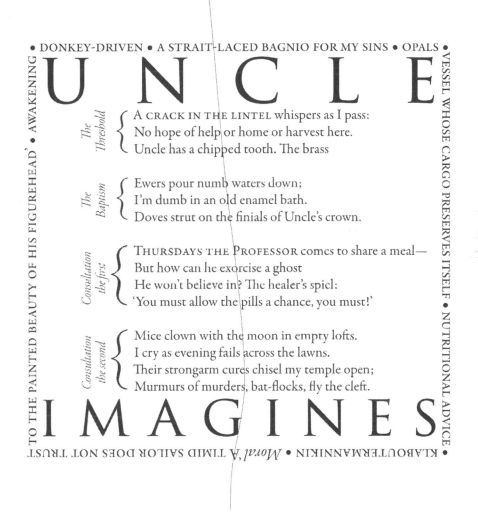

• DONKEY-DRIVEN • A STRAIT-LACED BAGNIO FOR MY SINS • OPALS •

U N C L E

The Threshold
{
A CRACK IN THE LINTEL whispers as I pass:
No hope of help or home or harvest here.
Uncle has a chipped tooth. The brass

The Baptism
{
Ewers pour numb waters down;
I'm dumb in an old enamel bath.
Doves strut on the finials of Uncle's crown.

Consolation the first
{
THURSDAYS THE PROFESSOR comes to share a meal—
But how can he exorcise a ghost
He won't believe in? The healer's spiel:
'You must allow the pills a chance, you must!'

Consolation the second
{
Mice clown with the moon in empty lofts.
I cry as evening fails across the lawns.
Their strongarm cures chisel my temple open;
Murmurs of murders, bat-flocks, fly the cleft.

I M A G I N E S

KLABOUTERMANNIKIN • 'A TIMID SAILOR DOES NOT TRUST' • *Moral*

(left margin, vertical) AWAKENING 'TO THE PAINTED BEAUTY OF HIS FIGUREHEAD'

(right margin, vertical) VESSEL WHOSE CARGO PRESERVES ITSELF • NUTRITIONAL ADVICE •

GOLD & GANGUE • CURARE CEREMONIAL • MY UNSPEAKABLE OBEDIENCE •

FLAT ROOF *of the* TEMPLE • TO PULL DOWN THEIR FOLKLORIC HEARTS

WHO OR HOW OR WHAT MAKES ME A BROTHER TO VIOLENCE'

F O L K

The sun observing the planets

SCRAP OF LAWN outside the kindergarten.
I returned.
          The foul weather abated. A crocus,
A plait of bread rising in a dingy wood.

The crow observing the deer

I knelt among the birches and lay down and vomited
And slept.
          Calm, serious voices. The little leaves
Dark and restless against a blue and airy sky—

Theory of modern medicine

KEEP ME HERE under the trees, my homeland!
My brown heart's seismic stone—peripheries—
The webs of leaves shaking benedictions.
A wet conclave of earth and stone.

Alternative theory

Prone to the laws of season, when I was very close
I flew far distant, and awoke—forgetful—
Raving—a sunflower, blinded by finches,
Torn from its merry scrap of ground.

S O N G

CLOUDFORMS OR TURBULENCE WITHIN ONE • *Plaint,* CAN'T SAY •

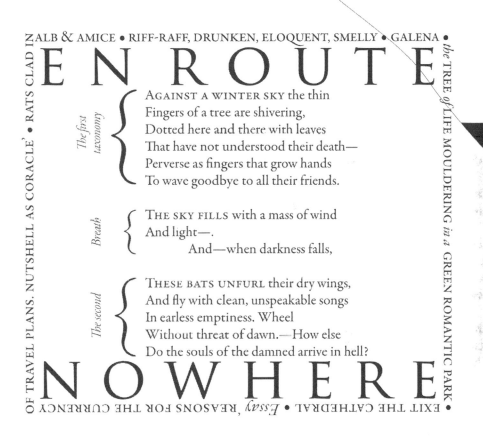

EN ROUTE

The first taxonomy

AGAINST A WINTER SKY the thin
Fingers of a tree are shivering,
Dotted here and there with leaves
That have not understood their death—
Perverse as fingers that grow hands
To wave goodbye to all their friends.

Breath

THE SKY FILLS with a mass of wind
And light—.
            And—when darkness falls,

The second

THESE BATS UNFURL their dry wings,
And fly with clean, unspeakable songs
In earless emptiness. Wheel
Without threat of dawn.—How else
Do the souls of the damned arrive in hell?

NOWHERE

Border text: OF TRAVEL PLANS. NUTSHELL AS CORACLE' • RATS CLAD IN ALB & AMICE • RIFF-RAFF, DRUNKEN, ELOQUENT, SMELLY • GALENA • *the* TREE *of* LIFE MOULDERING *in a* GREEN ROMANTIC PARK • EXIT THE CATHEDRAL • 'REASONS FOR THE CURRENCY, *Essay*

KING OF

the HABITAT • THE BEETLE'S ELEGIAC VISIONS • LIGHT & WATER

'STEADILY, STEADILY, ACROSS THE GREAT GRAVE BLOWS?' • PRAYER

The Night

SPENT THE NIGHT in the woods, in a blanket of crumbling
Bark, shivering, safely far from the house:
Worth chastisement and the sodden stumbling
To wake and walk with mind and stomach bare
Over the ridge to watch the morning rise
Without key-sound or the damned choir
Protesting at breakfast. Worth the tiredness and tears

The Morning

To STAND SOAKED among the hawthorns and look
East across a mile of withered beans,
Fuel for next year's crop on the rolling slope,
And see the fine rain greying out their black,
Coming towards us as the sky lightens,
Coming towards us at the end of another trance,
Coming towards me I won't let it stop.

THE WOOD

Poet's Note: *These poems were imagined as a textual equivalent of the strange outsider art produced by some inmates of mental asylums in the early 20th century. Their obsessive formality could only lead to the sonnet. The use of a persona whose worldview was, to say the least, unreliable, turned out to liberate bits of myself that I had never before been able to formulate in words. Each page is to be imagined as a ceramic tile, smashed and then put back together to recover the original design.*

BIOGRAPHIES

Phil Brown teaches English in Sutton and has been regularly writing poetry for about ten years. In 2009 he was shortlisted for the Crashaw Prize and won the Eric Gregory Award in 2010. He has had his work published in *Magma, Pomegranate, Dove Release: New Flights and Voices* (Worple Press, ed. David Morley), Dr. Rhian Williams' *The Poetry Toolkit* (2009, Continuum), and the *Salt Collection of Young British Poets* (ed. Roddy Lumsden), *Lung Jazz: Young British Poets for Oxfam* (ed. Kim Lockwood and Todd Swift) and *Coin Opera 2* (ed. Jon Stone). He is the Poetry Editor for the online magazine and chapbook publisher, Silkworms Ink. His debut collection, *Il Avilit*, was published by Nine Arches Press in 2011.

Peter Carpenter is co-director of Worple Press (find out more at www.worplepress.co.uk); his 'New and Selected' poems, *Just Like That* was published by Smith/Doorstop in 2012, following five previous collections; subsequent work has appeared in journals including *Canto, Poetry Ireland Review, Blackbox Manifold, Tears in the Fence, The North* and *Agenda*. He is also an essayist, reviewer and a teacher of creative writing; 'Singing Schools and Beyond: the Roles of Creative Writing' appeared in *The Oxford Handbook of Contemporary British and Irish Poetry* (OUP 2013). Nine Arches Press published his collection, *After the Goldrush*, in 2009.

Tom Chivers was born in 1983 in South London. His publications include *How to Build a City* (Salt Publishing, 2009), *The Terrors* (Nine Arches Press, 2009; shortlisted for the Michael Marks Award) and, as editor, *City State, Adventures in Form* and *Mount London* (Penned in the Margins, 2009, 2012, 2014). In 2009 he presented a documentary for BBC Radio 4 on the poet Barry MacSweeney. In 2012 his poem 'The Event' was animated by Julia Pott for Channel 4. His work has been commissioned by the Bishopsgate Institute, Cape Farewell, Southbank Centre, London International Festival of Theatre and Humber Mouth Literature Festival. He is currently working on his second collection, *Dark Islands*, and on a book of creative non-fiction, *London Clay: A Journey into the Deep City*.

Myra Connell's first pamphlet, *A Still Dark Kind of Work*, was published by Heaventree Press in 2008, and her second, *From the Boat*, by Nine Arches Press in 2010. Her short fiction appeared in the Tindal Street Press collections, *Her Majesty* (2002), and *Are you she?* (2004). She lives in Birmingham, where she combines writing with working as a psychotherapist.

Claire Crowther has published two full collections (the first of which was shortlisted for the Aldeburgh prize for Best First Collection), and three pamphlets, including *Mollicle* (Nine Arches Press, 2010). Her work appears in such journals as *Poetry Review* and *New Statesman* and she reviews regularly for, among others, *Poetry London*. She lives in Somerset but grew up in Hobs Moat, a small but magical area of Solihull.

Angela France has had poems published in many of the leading journals, in the UK and abroad and has been anthologised a number of times. She has an MA in Creative and Critical Writing from the University of Gloucestershire and is studying for a PhD. Publications include *Occupation* (Ragged Raven Press) and *Lessons in Mallemaroking* (Nine Arches Press). Angela is features editor of *Iota* and runs a monthly poetry cafe, 'Buzzwords'. Her latest collection, *Hide*, was published by Nine Arches Press in 2013.

Andrew Frolish was born in Sheffield in 1975. After studying politics at Lancaster University, he trained to be a teacher in the Lake District. His poems have been published in a variety of magazines, including *PN Review, Acumen, Envoi, Tears in the Fence, The Interpreter's House, Pulsar, Iota, Orbis* and *The Agenda Broadsheet*. He has received prizes in several competitions and won the Suffolk Poetry Society Crabbe Memorial competition in 2006. His poems for children have been published by Hopscotch. He now lives with his family in Suffolk, where he is a headteacher. *Retellings* (Nine Arches Press 2012) is his debut collection.

Roz Goddard co-ordinates the West Midlands Readers' Network, an organisation that works extensively with libraries and readers' groups, produces reading events and commissions new work from regional writers. She is also a poet and short-fiction writer. She has published four collections of poems, the most recent *The Sopranos Sonnets and Other Poems* (Nine Arches Press, 2010) featured on Radio 3's The Verb and her work is on permanent display in Birmingham Museum and Art Gallery. She is currently working on a new collection of poems to be published in 2014. Examples of her poetry and fiction can be found here: www.rozgoddard.com.

After Anglican priesthood, theatre reviewing and years at West Midlands Arts, **David Hart** has worked freelance as a poet, for several busy years with poetry work out there, and now several books and pamphlets later working alone, apart from a period of eventual disillusionment as Library of Birmingham Poet, during the transition from the Central Library, 2012-13, of which poems, he says, will speak as and when. *The Titanic Café closes its doors and hits the rocks* was published by Nine Arches Press in 2009 and shortlisted for the Michael Marks pamphlet prize.

Luke Kennard won an Eric Gregory award in 2005 for his first collection of prose poems *The Solex Brothers* (Stride Books). His second collection of poetry *The Harbour Beyond the Movie* was shortlisted for the Forward Prize for Best Collection in 2007 making him the youngest poet ever to be nominated for the award. His criticism has appeared in *Poetry London* and *The Times Literary Supplement*. He is currently reviewing fiction for

The National. In 2011, Nine Arches Press published Kennard's poem-play sequence, *Planet-Shaped Horse*, as a pamphlet.

Milorad Krystanovich was born in 1950 in Dalmatia, then part of the former Yugoslavia. He studied at Split University before becoming a teacher and came to the UK in 1992 after conflict engulfed the region. He later joined The Cannon Poets, becoming a founder member of Writers Without Borders and an active and well-respected figure within Birmingham's poetry and writing community. Hailed by Jonathan Morley in 2007 as "Birmingham's finest émigré poet", Milorad's published work includes three volumes published by Writers Without Borders and Heaventree Press published a bilingual pamphlet and his collection *The Yasen Tree* (2007). His penultimate volume, *Improvising Memory* (from which the poems in this anthology have been taken), was published by Nine Arches Press in 2010. Milorad also taught at the Brasshouse Language Centre in Birmingham and wrote numerous plays and novels for children and young people. Milorad Krystanovich died in September 2011, and a collection of poems, *Moses' Footprints,* was published posthumously by Nine Arches Press in 2012.

Ruth Larbey was born in Cyprus, and grew up in Nottingham, Hong Kong and rural Cumbria. She has spent her last two years working in London, after completing her MA at Warwick University in 2008. She has been published in various magazines, and organises music and art performance events in her spare time. *Funglish* (Nine Arches Press, 2010) is her debut pamphlet of poems.

Chris McCabe was born in Liverpool in 1977. His poetry collections are *The Hutton Inquiry, Zeppelins* and *THE RESTRUCTURE* (all Salt Publishing). In 2013, he published a London poetry collaboration with Jeremy Reed, *Whitehall Jackals*, with Nine Arches Press. He has recorded a CD with The Poetry Archive and written a play *Shad Thames, Broken*

Wharf, which was performed at the London Word Festival and subsequently published by Penned in the Margins in 2010. He works as Poetry Librarian at The Poetry Library, London, and teaches for The Poetry School.

Matt Merritt is a poet and wildlife journalist from Leicester. His third and most recent collection, *The Elephant Tests,* is published by Nine Arches Press, and previous publications include *hydrodaktulopsychicharmonica* (Nine Arches Press, 2010), *Troy Town* (Arrowhead, 2008), and *Making The Most Of The Light* (HappenStance, 2005). He blogs at polyolbion.blogspot.co.uk

David Morley's most recent collection of poems, *The Gypsy and the Poet,* was published by Carcanet Press in 2013, to be followed next year by *Biographies of Birds and Flowers: Selected Poems.* He writes for *The Guardian* and *Poetry Review.* He judged the 2013 T.S. Eliot Prize and is also judging this year's Foyles Young Poets Award. Nine Arches Press published his pamphlet, *The Night of the Day,* in 2009.

Alistair Noon was born in 1970 and grew up in Aylesbury. Besides time spent in Russia and China, he has lived in Berlin since the early nineties, where he works as a translator. His poetry and translations from German and Russian have appeared in nine chapbooks from small presses. *Earth Records* (Nine Arches Press, 2012) is his first full-length collection.

Matt Nunn is a poet and creative writing tutor and the author of three poetry collections, *Apocalyptic Bubblegum* (MAP 2002), *Happy Cos I'm Blue* (Heaventree Press, 2007) and *Sounds in the Grass* (Nine Arches Press, 2009). He lives in Solihull with his wife and two children.

Mario Petrucci's work is "vivid, generous and life-affirming" (*Envoi*). His most recent poems, inspired by Black Mountain and hailed as "modernist marvels" (Poetry Book Society), embrace contemporary issues of searing social and personal relevance via a distinctive combination of innovation and humanity. Through ground-breaking residencies, poetry films and a remarkable output of eco-poetry, his unique scientific sensibility has tirelessly illuminated the linguistic as well as emotive resonances of love and loss in the public and private domains. Whether exploring the tragedies of Chernobyl (*Heavy Water,* 2004) or immersing himself in heart-rending invention (*i tulips,* 2010), Petrucci aspires to "Poetry on a geological scale" (*Verse*). His latest collection is *anima* (Nine Arches Press, 2013).

Jeremy Reed has been for decades one of Britain's most dynamic, adventurous and controversial poets; *The Independent* called him "British poetry's glam, spangly, shape-shifting answer to David Bowie". He has published over 40 books of poetry, fiction and non-fiction, winning prizes such as the Somerset Maugham Award. His poetry publications in recent years include *Heartbreak Hotel* (Orion), *Duck and Sally Inside, This Is How You Disappear* (both Enitharmon), *West End Survival Kit* (Waterloo Press), *Bona Drag* (Shearsman) and *Piccadilly Bongo* with Marc Almond (Enitharmon), and his most recent novels are *The Grid* (Peter Owen) and *Here Comes the Nice* (Chomu Press). Jeremy Reed also performs with musician Itchy Ear as The Ginger Light. His latest collection is a collaboration with Chris McCabe, *Whitehall Jackals* (Nine Arches Press, 2013).

Daniel Sluman is based in Gloucestershire. His poems have appeared widely in journals such as *Cadaverine, Popshot, Shit Creek Review,* & *Orbis*. He is the poetry editor of *Dead Ink*, and is on the editorial board for *Iota*. His debut full-length collection, *Absence has a weight of its own*, was published in 2012 by Nine Arches Press.

Maria Taylor is a Leicestershire-based poet. Her debut collection, *Melanchrini*, was published by Nine Arches Press in 2012. Her writing has been published in *The North, The Guardian, The TLS, Staple* and others. http://miskinataylor.blogspot.co.uk

Simon Turner has written two collections of poetry, the most recent of which, *Difficult Second Album*, was published by Nine Arches Press in 2010. His poems have appeared in a variety of publications, both in print and online, including *Tears in the Fence, The Wolf*, and *Poetry Salzburg;* work is forthcoming in *PN Review* and *Poetry Wales*. *Works on Paper*, a pamphlet, is due from Seren in 2014.

Deborah Tyler-Bennett is author of five poetry collections, the most recent being *Kinda Keats* (Shoestring, 2013), poems based on a residency at Keats House. Others are *Mytton... Dyer... Sweet Billy Gibson...* (Nine Arches, 2011), *Revudeville* (King's England, 2011), *Pavilion* (Smokestack, 2010), and *Clark Gable in Mansfield* (King's England, 2003). Her first volume of short stories *Turned Out Nice Again: Stories Inspired by the Music Hall Tradition* is out from King's England Press (2013). She regularly performs her work.

Tony Williams's *All the Rooms of Uncle's Head* (Nine Arches Press, 2011) was a Poetry Book Society Pamphlet Choice. He also writes prose fiction, and teaches creative writing at Northumbria University. His new collection of poems, *The Midlands*, is forthcoming from Nine Arches Press in 2014.

ACKNOWLEDGEMENTS

Sincere thanks are due to the following organisations and individuals for their support, kindness and enthusiasm both for this anthology, and for Nine Arches' various poetry and publishing endeavours over the last five years:

Jo Bell, Matt Nunn, Simon Thirsk and Neil Astley at Bloodaxe Books, Jonathan Davidson, Sara Beadle and all at Writing West Midlands, Sophie O'Neill, Emily Tate and Rebecca Robinson at Inpress, Jonathan and Maria Taylor at Crystal Clear Creators, Ceri Gorton, Helena Nelson, Rachael Ogden, the Warwick Writing Programme, and last but by no means least, Kevin Brook.

Many thanks to Cathy Perry for kind permission to reproduce Milorad Krystanovich's poetry, and to Carcanet and Michael Schmidt for permission to reproduce a selection of David Morley's poems, which also appear in *Enchantment* (Carcanet, 2010).

Thanks are due to the brilliant poets we have been so fortunate to have worked with over the last five years, and who have been at the heart of everything Nine Arches has been about. Additional thanks for their kind permission to reproduce their work in this anthology.

And finally, to our readers – where would we be without you?

FORTHCOMING FROM NINE ARCHES PRESS IN 2014

Debut New Poets collections:

Josh Ekroy – *Ways to Build a Roadblock*

This is a debut of adroit and concise poems, observed from the standpoint of an unflinching witness to the 'shock and awe' of early twenty-first century history. A startling collection with an illuminating and satirical energy.
Published: May 2014 **ISBN:** 978-0-9927589-0-5 **Price:** £8.99

Richie McCaffery – *Cairn*

An understated but quietly brilliant collection of poems, where each well-chosen word is luminous and fresh as a beach-combed pebble; these are poems you'll want to pocket, treasure and keep close to your heart.
Published: June 2014 **ISBN:** 978-0-9927589-1-2 **Price:** £8.99

Mark Burnhope – *Species*

This first full collection by Mark Burnhope brings both wrath and wryness to bear on inequality, ignorance and prejudice. *Species* is radical and acutely aware – a rare and brilliant mix that makes for essential and important poetry.
Published: June 2014 **ISBN:** 978-0-9927589-2-9 **Price:** £8.99

Under the Radar magazine:

A regular magazine showcasing some of the best poetry and short stories from new and established writers. A place for discoveries for readers and writers alike. See website for information.

Find out more about Nine Arches Press at:
www.ninearchespress.com